S0-EAQ-794

Piece Work

Drama Series 14

Miriam Packer

PIECE WORK

A Play

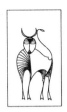

Guernica

Toronto / New York / Lancaster
1997

Copyright © 1997, Miriam Packer
and Guernica Editions Inc.
All rights reserved.
Printed in Canada.

Typeset by Selina, Toronto.
The Publisher gratefully acknowledges support
from The Ontario Arts Council and The Canada Council.
Antonio D'Alfonso, Editor
Guernica Editions Inc.
P.O. Box 117, Station P, Toronto (On), Canada M5S 2S6
250 Sonwill Drive, Buffalo, N.Y. 14225-5516 U.S.A.
Gazelle, Falcon House, Queen Square, Lancaster LR11RN
U.K.
Legal Deposit — Third Quarter
National Library of Canada.
Library of Congress Catalog Card Number: 95-81761
Canadian Cataloguing in Publication Data
Packer, Miriam
Piece Work
(Drama series ; 14)
A play.
Includes some text in French.
ISBN 1-55071-038-9
I. Title. II. Series.
PS8581.A26P53 1996 C812'.54 C95-920950-6
PR9199.3.P276P53 1996

Characters

SARAH

A woman of sixty-five, the oldest worker in the shop. She is of Russian-Yiddish origin, and she has the distinct idiom and accent of the small Russian village or shtetl. Sarah has an expressive intelligent face; her eyes are bright with wisdom and sparkle with her highly developed sense of humour. She is something of the story-teller, often commenting on the dynamics of the group or carefully integrating the pieces of a character's life, including her own. She has a highly developed sense of curiosity about the design of individual lives — Goldie's, Juanita's, Huguette's, Olga's, and her own. Sarah obviously enjoys the sense of community which she shares with the other workers. She reacts strongly to injustice, and often functions as pacifier in an attempt to restore a sense of peace and justice in the group.

HUGUETTE

A meek French-Canadian woman in her early forties, vulnerable and sad at times. Huguette is the most obvious scapegoat in the shop's social and psychological politics. Often bullied by the other women, Huguette confides most in Sarah, speaking in broken English with many French phrases thrown in, and Sarah responds in her own broken English with a distinct Yiddish accent.

OLGA

A stockily-built Ukrainian woman of about fifty-five. Olga is a real fighter, capable of being fierce, but she is a likeable character, softened by Sarah's warmth and, of all the workers, perhaps closest to

Sarah. The friendship between Sarah and Olga means a great deal to both women.

JUANITA
A woman of West Indian origin, about twenty-seven years old. Juanita is slangy in her speech, openly assertive and jealous of Mimi, the one woman of about her own age who seems to be achieving more status and recognition than Juanita. She is capable of rather vulgar explosive outbursts and confrontations. Nevertheless, she reveals a definite sense of gentle warmth, humour, fair play, and a love of life.

MIMI
A lively young French woman of about twenty-five, coquettish, warm-spirited, vivacious. Very fluent in English, she speaks with a slight Parisian-sounding accent. Mimi, the prettiest and youngest woman in the shop, is obviously having an affair with Mr. Davis, the shop owner . . . an affair which is the source of much gossip. She definitely holds a higher status in the shop than do the other women. Mimi works as the boss's assistant and part-time secretary, and as such she functions as unofficial part-time forelady. Mimi is very often in the work room, distributing work and communicating the boss's orders to the women when he is too busy to do so himself. When she is not distributing work, she sits apart from the other women, in the boss's office, doing routine clerical work. She is better dressed and slightly more sophisticated than the other women.

GOLDIE
An unpleasant-looking, mean-spirited woman of about forty, the most angry of all the workers. She has been working in this factory much longer than any of the women — for twenty-one years; she clings to her territorial rights with an obsessive

spirit which borders on madness. She is very involved in concocting plots to damage a fellow worker and generally is instrumental in the system of scapegoating which often goes on in the factory. Goldie seems to be incapable of laughter and constructive communication with her fellow workers, and clearly has difficulty in celebrating the small moments of enjoyment which unify the workers as a community. Her most significant features are those of brittle rigidity, anger, bitterness, and insecurity. Though Sarah reaches out to Goldie with warmth, Goldie seems to be unable to trust warmth for any sustained period of time. She retreats to her pattern of hostility and bitterness again and again during the action of the play.

MR. DAVIS

The owner of the shop. A slim, well-dressed man of about fifty, affluent-looking, well-preserved, handsome. A man with a definite sense of personal vanity and a definite air of authority. Although he addresses the women in patronizing tones, he attempts to be pleasant to them. In spite of these attempts, Mr. Davis often loses control and, in times of pressure, he resorts to bullying. He is threatened by any show of united strength on the part of the women; at critical times, he attempts to divide them by turning them against one another.

Act One

Lights brighten on the cluttered work room of a garment factory. A number of ladies' coats of different colours are hung on garment racks. There are five work tables and accompanying chairs in the room set close together, each table cluttered with various buttons, pins, spools of thread, the odd scissors and the personal belongings of each worker — a coffee cup, a thermos bottle perhaps, and a special cushion on one or two of the chairs. The women work as finishers sewing finishing touches to the garments by hand. On one side of the room is an old sink. A mirror is tacked to the wall above it. There might be a few small windows looking out on a grim commercial building suggestive of the claustrophobic atmosphere of the work room. There might also be a small portable fan in a corner of the room to suggest the intense heat in summer. On one side of the room, visible to the audience, is an opening to the boss's office where Mimi — the boss's general assistant in the work room and part-time office girl — may sometimes work. It is early morning. Sarah, a short chubby woman with sparkling eyes, walks heavily into the empty room of the garment factory. She is dressed for winter, and puffs from the exertion of a walk through the snow. She carries her handbag and two shopping bags decorated with Christmas slogans. She is covered with snow, and stomps snow from her boots.

SARAH

Olga! Olgale! You're here?

Speaks aloud to herself as she shuffles over to her work-table.

Noo! So today I'm here earlier than Olga. Humph! Like in a race.

Placing her shopping bag on the floor, she rummages around in her purse.

Oi, did I forget? No, no . . . Here's the sharp scissors.

Places them on the table.

And here's the thimble.

Places it on the table.

Thank God, I remembered!

She hangs up her coat, and carefully takes a dress and folded cardigan out of her shopping bag. She hangs them up.

Oi, my back . . .

OLGA

Walks in heavily, stomping snow off her boots.

Ah, Sarooshka! Now, you talk-et to self? Yah! Yah! Ees factory make-et me crazy like dis too.

Laughs, dropping her bags heavily at her work-table.

SARAH

Oi, Olgale! I opened the purse and I couldn't find my scissors, so I got right away nervous. When it starts here a business with faster-faster — you need already two sharp scissors.

OLGA

Unpacking her large bag, takes out a thermos bottle, a sandwich, a huge orange.

Yah! Yesterday not have-et even minute to take break, ah?

Continuing to unpack — a sweater, a smock, scissors.

Yah — and-t dis Golda and Juanita make-et yesterday beeg trouble, ah?

Stops to illustrate yesterday's frenzy by gesturing. Pulls and grabs at an imaginary coat, while she talks.

Gimme coat!

Grabs.

Gimme coat sh-mall size!

Tugs.

Gimme coat beeg size! Ach!

Wags her head in disapproval.

Today, if make-et bother me — I gif good knock . . . vit hanger in head, Sarooshka. Yah?

Laughs, illustrating the blow she'll deliver.

SARAH
Laughing.

Sure, Olgale, sure . . .

OLGA
Goes over to the hanger to put away her coat.

All-a-time, me better ticket.

Tugs.

Me more ticket.

Pulls.

Me more monye. Ach!

SARAH
Arranging needles on her table, carefully setting up different coloured threads in place, smiles.

Oi, Olgale, with the piece-work business, it's always the same craziness, no? You finish a coat, you give a tear off the ticket, you get excited. You made maybe fifty cents for the piece. You tear off the second ticket — more excited! A dollar already! So now — can you take a rest? No! You want more!

Laughs.

OLGA
Yah, yah. Ees like one drunk man!

SARAH
Like eating strudel, Olga. You eat one little strudel, you want a second. Even if you're not already hungry — you take a third.

OLGA
Hangs up her party clothes. Laughs with Sarah.
Yah, ees all-a-time more strudel vant. Me too, Sarah.

SARAH
But, Olgale, here lately it's becoming like a war! Sometimes I want to cry already from nerves!

OLGA
Arranging things on table.
Ees true, Sarooshka. Yesterday mine head-d break-et!
Searching among her things.
I haf now to find mine glasses. Ven boss come, mine hands shake-et.

SARAH
You know, Olga, when I was a young girl straight from the boat, there, you know, on Main Street — it was different. I don't know exactly what...

OLGA
Still busy arranging things on table.
Ach, Sarooshka. Main Street ees for you first job in new country, ya? Ees different, ya!

SARAH
The garment business was full of the young immigrants, it's true. All of us together.

OLGA

Boss make-et scream plenty to young-k girl from old-country too, Sarah! Not forget!

SARAH

Sure . . . plenty troubles. Easy work it wasn't. But you know, Olga, we had together an enjoyment. I don't know exactly . . . We were sending home money to bring over here our parents, we were running to night school . . . America! It was a life!

OLGA

Yah — and young-k girl look-et all-a-time to find young-k man for marry! You too, Sarooshka?

SARAH

Oi, we used to run, Olga, with the little brown pay envelopes on a Friday night to a dance there from the young immigrants . . . So happy, like millionaires. Everything, Olga, we did together. Now it's something different. Who knows? Could be older is already different. Maybe this my David is saying to me.

OLGA

Sarooshka! You go yesterday to David's house, yah?
Starts to thread needles for the day. Puts on her glasses.
I make now ready needle.

SARAH

Threading her needle as well.
Sure, me too.
They thread silently for a second.

OLGA

Yah, Sarooshka. Tell me. Beeg lady make again deleever from delicatessen?
Scoffs.

SARAH

Oi, sure, leave it to my daughter-in-law. Sheila with
the hair-in-the-sky and the manicured nails. Again
she catered. Why not? Like us? She's afraid she'll,
God forbid, take off the nail polish if she puts her
hands into water to cook something.

OLGA

Ha, ha, ha. Ees order again blintzes, Sarah? Hah!
Hah! Ees not can make at home chop leever, dis
Sheilya? Hah! Ees not can make potato efen!
Leaning forward, looking over her glasses.
Ees yit still only banana? Hah!

SARAH

Yes, sure, Sheila with the cottage cheese and banana
diet and the exercise-shmexercise. A whole life she's
on a diet.
Sighs.
But it's . . .

OLGA

Sarooshka, make-et you something nervous, dis
Sheilya?

SARAH

Oi, Olgale. Her I don't care already. No, it was my
David upset me.

OLGA

He tell you something bad?

SARAH

Plenty bad, Olga. I was telling him from here stories,
you know. How he makes us run, Mr. Davis —
faster, faster — like horses sometimes. So all of a
sudden, my David says, 'Ma, you have to stop working! Sheila and I talked about it.'

OLGA

Ees tell you stop?

14

SARAH

'Sheila and I decided,' he says. 'You're too old to work.' This is what he says!

OLGA

Ees say 'too old-t,' Sarooshka? N'yet! Ees not haf respect for mäder.

SARAH

Sure, it's very easy to say! Sheila with the hair-in-the-sky . . .

Indicates elaborate hairdo.

. . . and him — they became over me a jury! He was just a young boy complaining that he couldn't play very good with the baseball there, and all of a sudden he's a whole manager!

OLGA

And how he tell you make monye, Sarooshka? Ees not beeg, pension for old-t people, ah?

SARAH

For this he has an answer too! 'Ma,' he says, 'you can stay with the children. We'll pay you.' By him it's good I should sit in the house all day and talk to the grandchildren — which they want anyways to play by themselves.

OLGA

N'yet! You not can seet een house like old babüshka.

SARAH

'You could even come live with us,' he says, like I'm already running to live by him.

OLGA

N'yet! Live een same house mit son and-t vife, ees come beeg trouble . . .

SARAH

I tried to explain . . . 'What, Davidel, am I going to do all day?'

Stops threading.
'Talk on the telephone? Go to a club there from the golden age? Draw pictures from the grandchildren?'
'Live by you in the basement under the stairs?'

OLGA
Wagging her head.
Een old-t country old-t lady live by children. All-a-time sit near stove vit black scarf over head-t, yah.
Imitates a little old lady passively and mutely sitting.
You not old-t lady, Sarooshka!

SARAH
I told him: 'Davidel, I go into work, I hear a song, I talk to a person . . . it makes an interest.'

OLGA
And you need monye.

SARAH
Sure, this too. With the pension alone — Oi vey, troubles.

OLGA
You tell heem no, Sarah?

SARAH
Sure, I told him no. So then Sheila opens a mouth to give also an opinion. She's also a specialist! And it comes out the real reason.

OLGA
Vat ees?

SARA
'It's not right for you to work in a factory,' she says. 'It's a shame,' she says. 'David is a professional man. You should consider him!'

OLGA

You tell her mind-t your own business, you! You
not . . .

SARAH

Interrupts.

So I looked to David, to hear him say something
smart . . . so instead he says the same thing like her!
Can you believe?

OLGA

Vat say-et?

SARAH

'People talk, Ma,' he says. 'I am a lawyer, after all.'
he says. 'It doesn't look right. And Sheila doesn't
like it.'

Waving her hands.

It's by them an embarrassment that his mother
works in a factory!

OLGA

From factory vork, ees fäder send heem to univer-
sitye, no?

*Angry, she gets up and pulls her smock jerkily
over her head.*

Very fast forget, ah?

SARAH

And afterwards — Sheila gives an example. 'My
mother doesn't work,' she says . . . like I have to do
everything what her mother does.

OLGA

Vat do-et, mäder?

SARAH

I was burning already — so I asked her. 'What does
your mother do all day, tell me?' So she tells me, she
plays a lot golf. You hear, Olga?

Speaks mockingly.

She stands with a little stick in a field there, and she knocks . . .

Pronounces the 'k'.

. . . a little ball all day! This is her job, Olga!

OLGA
Laughs.

Yah! Yah! I see-et een television, Sarah! Yah! Have leetle hat, yah?

SARAH
Yes. And the funny shorts.

Indicating quiet disapproval.

Old ladies with old knees in shorts!

OLGA
Yah, yah.

SARAH
So I told her. 'Very good. So your mother likes to knock there with the golf, so I like better to work! My business!'

OLGA
Goes back to threading needles.

You tell-et goot! You have for me black cotton?

SARAH
Sure, dear, sure.

Hands her the cotton. She gets up.

I better put on my smock. He'll come in soon.

Pulls the smock over her dress.

You know, he's a good boy, my David, but he cares maybe more for himself than for me . . .

OLGA
Ah, Sarooshka, children not care so much for mäder. N'yet! You not can seet een house like old-t lady and . . .

SARAH
Mournfully.

Like you take a bird, Olga, which it's older, you know, but it still flies. So you cut by it off the wings 'cause it's old, and then . . . it sits, like without wings already!

OLGA
Laughs huskily.
Ah, Sarooshka. You talk-et goot! You make me laugh all-a-time. N'yet, Sarah! N'yet! Me ant you . . . ees still young-k. Have big ving-ks, Sarah.
Flaps her arms and laughs.

SARAH
Laughs with her.
Oi, it's a pleasure. You see? My David is so serious, and his Sheila too! You sit with them for a night and they tell you: 'You're too old, Ma. It's not nice, Ma.' And you feel all of sudden to cry already.

OLGA
Clearing space on her table.
Sarooshka! Make-et ready now table for coat! To-day must be very fast.

SARAH
You're right. Today especially, with the Christmas party at one o'clock, we'll have to run here very fast!

OLGA
She continues to arrange her table.
Yah, yah! Like mine boy Alex! All-a-time make-et jogget! You know jogg-et?

SARAH
Yes, sure. They say it's good for the heart. Who knows?

OLGA
She starts to imitate the health conscious Alex.
Een a morning, jogget! Een a night, jogget. One, two, tree.

19

Hamming it up, laughing.
On head — vear little Schmate . . .
Indicates headband.
. . . like . . . uh . . . shtupid boy!
Huffing and puffing with exaggeration.
Jogget! Jogget! Jogget! Can haf one heart attack!
Enter Juanita and Goldie.

JUANITA
Hey, Olga, what you doin', girl? You the new long-
distance runner?

OLGA
Breathless and laughing.
Yah, yah — I make-et beeg exercise today, Juanita.

JUANITA
Well, get some practice. We are going to be hustlin'
our butts off in here.

SARAH
Golde, good morning, good morning dear.

GOLDIE
Grimly going to her work table.
What's so good about it anyways?

JUANITA
Moves about at her table.
Okay. Let me get my act together here.
Quickly arranges materials on her table.
Scissors, pins, buttons . . . Oh, yeah . . . snaps!
Goes off to a large side-table.
Hey, Sarah, where's Mimi keep those snaps, do you
know?

SARAH
Oi, there's no more snaps there? Golde, you have
extra snaps, dear?

OLGA
I go now in ladies' place.

20

GOLDIE
Very anxiously fussing.
I don't have extra anything. I'm busy here, can't you
see? I should of come in earlier.
Muttering.
Uch . . . I have to count my buttons for the day.
Yesterday I didn't count.

JUANITA
Hey, Goldie, you ain't gonna wear those winter
boots to the Christmas party, are you?

GOLDIE
T-s-k, leave me alone for a minute. I didn't have
time to take my boots off yet. Okay? Such a fuss
with a party! I came to work, not to go to a party!

JUANITA
Yeah . . . But, at one o'clock, the pumpkin turns into
Cinderella. Par-ty time! Ain't you brought some-
thin' special to wear?

SARAH
So it's okay. Maybe Golde wants to wear what she's
already wearing.

GOLDIE
What's the matter? You think I haven't got nice
clothes? You think I'm a welfare case or something?
I have my dress here, don't worry, Sarah.

SARAH
No . . . no. Who's worrying? I just mean sometimes
a person wants to go to a party in a plain dress.

GOLDIE
Never mind plain. I have very nice dresses, don't
worry.

JUANITA
Anybody got those square buttons?

GOLDIE

I have just enough for today! Yesterday, I had much more in my box here.

SARAH

Going over to Juanita.

I have plenty square buttons. Here. I came in early like always with Olga. Soon I'll start to work.

GOLDIE

Not so soon, Sarah. Half past eight! That's the rule!

SARAH

No. No. I mean half past eight, I'll start.

GOLDIE

Tugging off her boots.

If I was smart, I'd hide my buttons at night—so some people . . .

Enter Huguette, breathless and anxious.

SARAH

Good morning, Huguette. Oi, you're breathing heavy, dear.

HUGUETTE

I wait too long today for my boy. E's cry this morning before school. I talk to him long time. *J'suis en retard.*

Starts rummaging through her bag, throwing her coat over her chair.

SARAH

I'll hang up your coat for you, Huguette.

Goes over to rack with Huguette's coat.

Don't worry, dear, you have time.

HUGUETTE

Okay . . . *Merci*, Sarah.

OLGA

Coming back from washroom, shouts out.

Ees goot colour dress, Huguette!

SARAH
Excited.
Oh, yes . . . look. Special for the party, Huguette?

HUGUETTE
Ah oui . . . merci, Sarah.
Fumbles with her sewing materials.
I must hurry now. We 'av to start soon, ah?

SARAH
Don't worry, dear.

OLGA
Juanita! You ready vork-et now?

JUANITA
Almost! Yeah. I just gotta lay out my needles here, that's all.

HUGUETTE
Ah non — I make too slow.

SARAH
Running over to help Huguette.
Here . . . I'm finished, so I'll help. So the cotton is here, and here's the scissors . . . Oi, Huguette it's a bit torn the dress here.

HUGUETTE
Lifting her arm to examine the rip.
Ah oui. . . Maybe I'm going to wear a sweater to the party, ah.
Looking in her purse again.
I have to find now *mes lunettes* . . .

SARAH
No, no . . . you won't have to wear a sweater, I could fix.
She looks around and calls out.
Golde, you have red cotton maybe?

GOLDIE
I just came in! What are you bothering me with red cotton?

HUGUETTE
No, no, Sarah. I don't 'av time now. I 'av to finish 'ere.

SARAH
So I'll get cotton, and later I'll fix.
Shouts.
Juanita, you have some?

JUANITA
Squinting over some needles she's threading, speaks without looking up.
Hang on. I gotta prepare one needle of each size today. Yesterday I got caught without any big ones, you know, and I had to wait till Mimi brought me one. And man, she made me wait! Okay! I'm done!
Looks up.
Need red?

SARAH
For Huguette's dress. Later, I'll sew.

JUANITA
Hey, I can sew it now if we hurry.

HUGUETTE
No, no — I 'av to make my needles now.

SARAH
Picking up a needle from Huguette's table.
I'll finish here, Huguette. You go, dear.

HUGUETTE
Getting up.
Ben, okay. You finish dat, Sarah.
She goes over to Juanita's table timidly.

JUANITA

Okay now. Let's see.

Examines the tear.

Yup, it's that seam right in here alongside your hip. Hold onto that side real tight, so I can stitch it right.

Huguette holds the top of the ripped seam tight.

Here.

Juanita unzips the back and slips her hand under Huguette's skirt to hold it straight while she stitches.

There!

She squats and begins stitching.

Don't think I'm bold, but I just got to poke around inside your dress.

SARAH

Shouts out.

Oi, Huguette, chew a piece of cotton, dear. They say it's bad luck, God forbid, if someone sews when you wear.

Juanita is just completing the sewing as Mr. Davis walks in. He sees the two women huddled together, Huguette chewing cotton and holding onto the ripped seam, Juanita squatting and poking around inside her dress, and Sarah watching intently from Huguette's work-table.

DAVIS

Good morning, ladies.

Sarah, Huguette and Juanita start giggling. Goldie snorts.

JUANITA

Now don't you worry, Mr. D. We ain't gone crazy and we ain't makin' love. Just fixin' a dress.

DAVIS

Okay, ladies. Let's get organized. Mimi is bringing in the first rack of coats, and that's gotta be finished

25

as soon as possible. We'll be bringing another big lot
after that, and the whole thing has got to be done by
one o'clock sharp. This is a rush job — so keep at it
steady.

JUANITA
You mean we're gonna do two whole sets before our
party?

DAVIS
That's right.

JUANITA
Are they the exclusive styles?

DAVIS
Let's not get too concerned with the styles, Juanita.
The main thing is to work very quickly . . . okay?
Shouts out.
Mimi! Could you bring the rack in now and distrib-
ute the Elite coats. Hurry up please!
In a lower voice.
And keep on top of things, Mimi.
Davis exits.

GOLDIE
Oh, it's the Elite styles, he says. I want to get a lot
of those. Those pay good.

JUANITA
Yeah . . . that's the good part. The bad part is that
he sneaks in a whole bunch of those cheap ones like
yesterday.

MIMI
Okay, ladies, here are the Elites mostly. I will give
them out to you.

JUANITA
Mumbles to herself.
Shee-it. When Mimi starts handin' them out, I never
get my share. That broad can't stand me.

GOLDIE

Mimi . . . I just want you to know that yesterday I didn't get hardly any good coats. Today, you should give me first, and enough too.

MIMI
Checking the coats.

Eh, eh, Goldie. There's enough here for everybody, *ma belle.*
Addresses everyone.

We have to work very fast, ah? To finish at one.

SARAH

Huguette, you want a good thimble? I brought for you . . . Very light.

HUGUETTE

Ben oui, Sarah. Merci. It 'elps me to sew more fast. Yesterday I'm not so fast. I get much nervous.

JUANITA

Alright! Let's roll now! Hurry up there, Mimi! We're cookin!
Sits down.

SARAH

Oi, it's an excitement today! Never mind David with the not-nice.

OLGA

Sarooshka, you not forget!
Flaps her arms, imitating a bird.

Ees beeg vingk, ah?

SARAH
Giggling.

Oi, yoy, yoy. Olga with the jokes.

HUGUETTE
Laughs.

Is good fun.

SARAH
Like Main Street.

GOLDIE
Mimi! Why don't we take our own coats already?
You're going too slow.

MIMI
Non, non. I bring you the first coat for each lady.
The rest is on the rack.
Starts distributing the coats.
Voilà, Huguette . . . Sarah, ma belle . . .

JUANITA
Hey, Mimi . . . don't be forgettin' me! Give me
some good coats girl, 'cause Davis likes my work.
Seductively.
He likes my stuff, don't you know.

MIMI
Okay, okay. Here, Juanita . . . for you.
Sarcastically.
With all my love! The queen of the factory. Ah?

JUANITA
Real funny, girl! I'm crackin' up, you notice.

GOLDIE
Hurry up, Mimi.
*The women start to sew. They work in silence,
very intent on the sewing, each woman with a
coat on her lap or on the work table.*

MIMI
Pushing an empty rack.
Eh, ladies, when you finish the first coat, you put it
on this rack, and take another one from that rack
there. *Vite!* We must finish by one.

JUANITA
Yeah, yeah, yeah . . . Push, push, push!

MIMI
Eh, don't blame me, Juanita. It's Mr. Davis tell me that, ah?

JUANITA
Alright. Cool it . . . Tell Davis I'm speedin' ahead! Just keep givin' us these good-payin' styles. Hey, Mimi , I'm out of those snaps. Fill up that box on the supply table there, will ya?
The women are all sewing now.

SARAH
It's a soft material today, it goes quite easy. By you too, Huguette? It's soft?

HUGUETTE
Oui, c'est doux là.
They work silently.

JUANITA
Yeah, this material gives. Hey, you usin' the big-sized needle, Olga?

OLGA
Yah, vit beeg needle, ees go faster.

GOLDIE
Anxious.
Oh, you're using the big size? I started with the medium-sized needle, 'cause Mr. Davis said once it makes a nicer finish. Why did I use the medium, eh? Now — you'll finish before me!

SARAH
I'm also using the medium needle, Golde! Don't worry. It comes out the same.

GOLDIE
What do I care what you're using? They're using the big to go faster! Hey, Juanita and Olga, you should really use the medium needle. He once said — it

makes a nicer finish, he said. You have to listen to him.

JUANITA
Oh, later for that! I want to make some bucks in here.

GOLDIE
He likes a neat finish . . . I'm telling you.

JUANITA
Yeah . . . well, give it to him just like he likes it.

OLGA
Ees goot liningk een dis style, ah Sarooshka?'

SARAH
Sure! You pay plenty for these coats in the store. My David's Sheila wears this style . . . with the big earrings which it could pull off by her the ears.

GOLDIE
Olga, you're supposed to use a smaller needle. You'll see; he'll be mad.

OLGA
Nefer mind-t sh-mall needle! You make-et fast, ees more monye for you.

GOLDIE
With my luck — if I use the big needle — he'll notice.

JUANITA
Hell, no. All he notices is green dollar bills. Hey, Olga, the snaps go about one inch from the border, right?

OLGA
Yah, yah, one eench.

HUGUETTE
Me, I don't 'av enough snaps, Sarah.

SARAH
On the table, dear.

HUGUETTE
Goes to supply table.
You want, Sarah?

SARAH
No, I have plenty, dear.

OLGA
Shouts out.
Huguette, you bring-k some for me?

JUANITA
Trying to arrange her coat on the table.
Wish I had a bigger table to spread this baby out . . .

SARAH
Sewing.
With the basting on the back collar — it's hard to reach.

HUGUETTE
Coming back with the snaps.
Voici! I bring for you.

OLGA
Taking the snaps from Huguette.
Yah, yah. Goot.

GOLDIE
Juanita, you're on the collar seam already? So fast? Sure . . . 'cause I'm stupid, I'm using the medium like he said. I always listen, t-sk, t-s-k . . .

OLGA
You hear-et? Mine boy told me — reats paper. Vun diplomät — beeg man . . .
Motions to indicate the status of the man in question.

JUANITA
Playfully interrupts.
Just how big is he, Olga?

OLGA
Not understanding the joke, continues.
. . . politics-man from goovernment peoples — vife run away from heem. I see-et on television too.

SARAH
On the television they showed? Today everything is everyone's business.

OLGA
Yah, yah. Ees go vit näder man.

JUANITA
Hell! Just 'cause he's some big shot, everyone's talkin' about it! Ain't never seen my mug on TV when my man walks out on me.
Gets up, turns her coat over.

OLGA
Yah, yah. Vife not vant heem no more. Kaput!

HUGUETTE
Mon dieu.

GOLDIE
Dieu! Dieu! All day you talk in here. My ears hurt. Be quiet. I have to work faster. Juanita, you're almost on your third or what?

JUANITA
Seated again.
That's me . . . Speedy Juanita.

SARAH
Sewing steadily.
Terrible! To throw away a husband just like an old schmäte? Feh!

HUGUETTE
C'est pas gentil, ça.

MIMI
*Who has been circling about the supply table
and has heard the story, tunes in playfully.*
Eh, don't forget, ladies. A woman needs a real man,
ah? Maybe he don't keep her warm at night, ah?

JUANITA
A word from the expert.
Gets up suddenly to go to rack.

OLGA
Laughs.
Yah, yah, Mimi. Ees maysbe not haf mooscle!
Flexes her arm muscle.
Hah! Must drink schnapps before sleep vit vife, no?
Make-et strong!
*Laughing, she goes off to hang one finished coat
up and to get another from rack.*

HUGUETTE
Mon dieu. C'est pas fin.

GOLDIE
Anxiously watching Olga going to the rack.
Dieu! Again *dieu!* You talk so much in here, my cot-
ton's stuck already.

OLGA
Ah, you don't know from notink politics, Golda!
Just monye, you know-et!

GOLDIE
You should talk! You already with the tenth coat
there. You come here from Europe, and buy a house
with my taxes!

OLGA
Never mind-t, you!

SARAH
Look! Mimi is wearing such a beautiful blouse. This would be a nice style for you too, Juanita . . .

MIMI
Eh, non. You could not afford that, Juanita. It's a gift. From Boutique Elle . . . Real silk.

JUANITA
That blouse ain't real silk!

MIMI
Oh, no? How do you know about that?

SARAH
You wear expensive clothes too, Juanita. Your winter coat is a beauty, dear.

JUANITA
Thanks, Sarah. My man got it for me . . . suede.

MIMI
I think, ladies, she gets her suede in the flea market.
Mimi saunters out of the room.

JUANITA
Damn, she's a phoney broad! Hell, even that there accent is phoney.
Mimics.
'Boutique Elle, ladeez . . . Real seelk, ladeez.' Shee-it! Thinks she's better than everyone else. Just cause she's hittin' the sac with Davis and got herself that cushy job.

SARAH
No, no, dear. Don't pay attention to the silk-shmilk. Some people are like that. They like to give a needle. Everything, they have better than you.

JUANITA
Oh yeah, that's her alright!

SARAH
Sewing.
It's like some of the ladies which they go to the golden age club to spend the afternoon.
Chuckles.
Oi . . . Starts there a competition. One lady says my son's a lawyer, so another says mine a doctor. One says my grandchildren are smart, so another says mine smarter.

JUANITA
The who's-on-top bullshit.

SARAH
One lady says my son is a specialist from the feet, so another says: 'Oi, from the feet? Nothing! My son is a specialist from the heart!'
Sighs.
I like better to mind my own business and work!

JUANITA
Yeah . . . right . . . don't pay them no never-mind!

SARAH
Oi, Olga. I forgot to ask. How is the basement doing by you?

OLGA
Ees finished. Ve make-et now special cäbinet for schnapps.

GOLDIE
At the coat rack, shouts out.
There's not so many of these Elite styles. There won't be enough for me. Does Mimi bring more of these styles, Juanita, or . . . ?

JUANITA
Hell, I don't know.
Juanita goes off to the bathroom.

OLGA

Yah, Sarah, mine Alex make-et party een basement for Christmas.

Mimi walks in again and begins to work at the supply table.

GOLDIE
At the rack, shouts.

Mimi, I won't have enough Elite coats. I'm taking two more for me now, okay?

Quietly.

For later, so I can catch up with them.

MIMI
Mechanically.

Okay, okay, Goldie.

Goldie goes back to her place with two coats. Starts to sew.

OLGA

For Christmas, ve have-et beeg par-ty. I bring here halooshkes after Christmas.

Looking down at her work.

I make-et seam more fast now.

SARAH

It's the first few stitches on the coat is always the hardest. I'll go already to take a fresh coat.

HUGUETTE

Me too, Sarah.

SARAH

Good, dear. So we'll hang up together.

Sarah and Huguette go off to the rack together. Juanita walks back into the room from the bathroom.

MIMI
Looking over the rack of finished coats.

They're going good, ladies, ah?

OLGA
Yah, yah!

MIMI
Okay, I'm going back to the office. If you need me . . .

JUANITA
Sarcastic.
Yeah! . . . We'll just call out your name, girl . . .
Mimi exits haughtily.

SARAH
Settling down in her seat again, starts sewing.
So, Huguette, you have already your Christmas tree?

HUGUETTE
Ah, Sarah, *mon dieu,* I 'av much trouble. *Mon mari est parti.* I 'av to buy presents for my kids. It's only one day before Christmas.

SARAH
So what will you do, Huguette?

HUGUETTE
I don't want my boys to cry, you know. They needs nice Christmas same like every boy.

SARAH
Maybe ask your sister, Huguette? Don't be shy.

HUGUETTE
Ah, j'sais pas. I don't like dat, to h'ask her. We get pay today, ah? I go fast tomorrow and make surprise for my little boys. They be very happy for Christmas.

OLGA
Getting up, rubbing her back.
Ach, now mine back hurt.

SARAH

In the meantime, I have for your boys, Huguette. From my grandchildren I have. Maybe you'll come to me tomorrow. It's only one bus. I'll give you with pleasure.

HUGUETTE

Ah, Sarah. You're good lady. You don't go to church, but you're *ben* good.

SARAH

Church-schmurch makes no difference. A person is a person. Oi, this seam is not so easy already!

JUANITA
Yells out from rack.

Hey, what's goin' on? I went to the john for a few minutes, and most o' the coats took a walk! Hey, Goldie, what ya doin'? Stackin' them away in your pants?

GOLDIE

I just took my share, that's all.

JUANITA

What you talkin' about . . . your share? Ah, what the hell? I ain't gonna mess with you today! It's Christmas. Whoee!
Takes a coat from the rack.

One more for me. Hey, you guys, you better pull your next coat, I'm tellin' ya. Goldie here is into storing these babies. She's hangin' em out the windows, I think.

OLGA
Absently.

Ees vat een vindow?

JUANITA

Alright . . .
Goes to radio.

38

Lemme turn on some music here.

She sits down, starts to sew and sings along comically.

'I'm dreamin' of a white Christmas . . .' Yup, can't wait to see my Santa . . . Just love to cuddle in his lap.

The Christmas music is heard softly in the background.

SARAH

So, Juanita, you also have a party for Christmas?

JUANITA

Yeah . . . I get together with my sisters 'n' brothers . . . and we party!

SARAH

You have brothers and sisters? Very nice. How many?

JUANITA
Howls.

Sarah, baby, you're a riot! I mean my people. My sisters and brothers are my friends.

SARAH

Well, sure . . . What better friends than brothers and sisters, tell me. Family is family.

Fanning herself, Olga gets up to open a window.

JUANITA

See I don't have blood family here. They're all back home.

SARAH

Oi, so you must be lonesome here.

JUANITA
A little sad.

Yeah, in a way. I miss 'em.

SARAH
This is terrible.

JUANITA
Yeah, but I'm makin' it.
Gets up, arranges her coat on the table.
Got my own place, my own job, and my own
friends. Yeah! And all these fine coats are goin' real
fast today.

SARAH
Sure, could be sometimes, friends could also be a
family. Could be here is more a family sometimes
than by my David. You know, Juanita, my boy
David . . .

GOLDIE
Enough talking, Sarah! All day you're talking.
Mimics.
'Family is family.' 'Friends is family.' Everything's
your business there!

HUGUETTE
It's good, Sarah . . . to talk. *C'est ben l' fun, ça.* Me,
I like dat. You know, my little boys, 'e's *ben smart.*

GOLDIE
Bristling.
Oh, look at that! Now Dummie there makes a re-
mark for a change! She's also got a speech from a
family. Look better at your coats, Huguette. I don't
want to know from your boys. I'm still behind here
with your cute little boys in the middle of everything!

JUANITA
Hey, can it, Goldie! Man, you're a bitch!

GOLDIE
Don't call me names, you. I could call you plenty.
Pauses, searching in her button box.

40

Now I'm missing the square buttons. What happened to my square buttons . . . what . . .

OLGA
Ah, you too much nervous all-a-time, Golda. Ees Mimi bring-et soon buttons.

GOLDIE
I don't want to wait for Mimi, okay? I had the special buttons right here. Who took them, I want to know.

Rummaging around very nervously looking for lost buttons.

It's probably Dummie-Huguette took them. She came here two months ago, and she's already stealing my buttons, I bet.

SARAH
It maybe fell down your buttons. Give a look . . .

GOLDIE
Ya, sure . . . fell down, sure.

She looks around on the floor nervously and quickly retrieves her buttons.

Okay, okay, I found them. It's 'cause you talk so much in here, I'm losing my buttons already.

JUANITA
Jesus, girl, you got buttons in that brain o' yours!

GOLDIE
And you? You don't have any brains at all! You come from the slums there . . . You probably took some of my buttons yourself.

JUANITA
Watch it, Goldilocks!

SARAH
Visibly upset.

Oi, oi. Such a fight here. Better maybe, like David says, to sit quietly at home and rest the nerves.

OLGA
Roars.
Ees cr-azy house here! Ve talk-et from par-ty . . . and
Golda make-et fight from buttons. Ees crazy lady!

GOLDIE
What do you know, you 'd.p.'? You took yourself
six pins from my pin-cushion last week. I saw you.

OLGA
Vat you talk-et? I take-et pins and bring-et back!

GOLDIE
Never mind! You're all finishing faster than me with
the big needles, so you think you're smart.
She gets up.
I'm going to put cold water on my face. Don't take
anything from my table there!
*She walks out very quickly, looking anxiously
back at her work-table.*

JUANITA
Man, that Goldie has got an ugly attitude, I'll tell
you.

SARAH
Oi sh — sh. Shah! 'Ugly' is not nice to say.

JUANITA
Well, hell! Let's tell it like it is, Sarah. What are ya
gonna call her? Sweet? With that sour puss on?
*She grimaces to imitate Goldie's sour expres-
sion.*

OLGA
Laughs.
Hah! hah! hah! Ees true. Golda ees funny-face.
Hah! Hah! Sarooshka? You tell me 'ees beauty, dis
Golda?

SARAH

No, no. I'm not going to tell a lie. She looks plenty mean, it's true. Always something mad. But . . .

OLGA

Ees funny face, no? Ees look like vun vitch-lady.

SARAH

Well . . . uh . . . pretty she's not. No! Not exactly pretty! But who knows why? Could be she's not happy inside, so she looks already not pretty.

Juanita and Olga laugh simultaneously.

OLGA

Roars with laughter.

Yah, yah. Ees Golda's nose come crook because she haf trouble much! Hah! Hah! Hah!

Olga and Juanita are still laughing as Goldie rushes back into the room from the bathroom.

GOLDIE

So you finished plenty while I was in the bathroom, I bet!

JUANITA

Yeah, yeah! We hit on gold! Hey, Olga found a diamond in the seam of her coat. Whyn't you rip up your seams, girl, so you find your diamonds? Hey . . . Davis won't mind.

GOLDIE

Very funny. You should be on stage you're so funny.

JUANITA

Yeah . . . I should be in the lights!

Mimi walks into the room at this point with a work-sheet in her hands.

MIMI

Okay, ladies. Settle down. The second lot is ready.

JUANITA
Hey, hold on! I haven't got a motor in me.

GOLDIE
Ya . . . wait. Gimme a chance to catch up with them.
It's not fair.
Davis walks in.

DAVIS
Turn off the radio for a minute, will you?
Pacing.
Is the last lot finished?

JUANITA
We're still workin' at 'em.

DAVIS
No, no. Too slow, ladies. Pick up the speed.
Starts checking the finished coats.
Okay. Each of you has one coat at your table, right?
Counts.
So with these that should add up to the whole lot.
Counts again.
This doesn't add up. We're missing two.
Agitated.
Where are the two extra coats here? Come on. I haven't got all day to play. Mimi, where are the extra coats? You're supposed to supervise here!

MIMI
But, Morton, I checked all morning.

DAVIS
Never mind 'Morton'. You call me Mr. Davis in here. Where the hell are those two coats?

GOLDIE
Quietly.
I still have two here.

DAVIS

Look, Goldie! If you want this job, follow orders, okay? Take one at a time. And move a little faster in here, everybody. We've got the whole second lot to finish by one o'clock.

JUANITA

We're going as fast as we can . . .

DAVIS

Well, you'll have to go faster. Okay. Hurry it up. Keep going. Remember, we don't have the Christmas party until both sets are done! Mimi, take Goldie's extras and give them to Olga and Juanita, will you?

GOLDIE

Why are you giving my coats to them? They're mine!

DAVIS

They're not yours! They go to whoever finishes them fastest.

JUANITA

Yeah . . . right. Whoever sweats the most gets the most! They don't call this the sweat shop for nothin'.

DAVIS

Mimi! Can I talk to you here please.

Exits and addresses her privately in the office away from the other women. Their conversation overlaps with the complaining voices of the women in the other room. Goldie's voice is heard shrilly in the background.

GOLDIE

You see? You talk in here and I get in trouble.

DAVIS

No, Mimi. It's your job to see that the work gets out fast. Olga's fast, and Juanita's very good.

Holds up his hand.

Never mind telling me she's not that good.

JUANITA
Overlapping.

Ah, stop complainin', Goldie.

DAVIS

This is a business and you're supposed to have business in mind when you're here. Keep them moving. Don't let them forget who's boss!

OLGA
Overlapping.

No, keep-et coat for you!

MIMI

But I'm not the boss, eh? I'm not even a real forelady.

GOLDIE
Overlapping.

You always get more anyways.

DAVIS

You have to keep telling them what to do. If you're too nice in there...

JUANITA
Overlapping.

Forget it, Goldie.

MIMI

They don't listen to me, because they don't know what I am. Me too, I don't know what I do. You should hear how they talk to me in there, because I'm not a forelady.

JUANITA
Overlapping.
What next? Five hundred horse blankets to sew?

DAVIS
Look, when you're in that room . . .

MIMI
If you want things to go smooth in there, you should make me the forelady for real, Morton.

DAVIS
Look, Mimi! Don't get upset today. Not today. Please, I have the whole second lot to get out. We'll talk about it another time.

MIMI
Sarcastically.
Oh, sure.

JUANITA
Hey, Mr. D.! When's the second lot coming?

DAVIS
Okay, go tell them about the budget styles now, Mimi, and do a good job, eh?

MIMI
Walking back into the centre of the room, puts on an air of relaxed superiority.
Okay, ladies, so you're almost finished, ah?

JUANITA
Yeah . . . So get the next lot ready for us, now, 'cause I ain't gonna be here till midnight.

MIMI
Eh there, don't be so smart with me, ah?

JUANITA
Gives Mimi a dirty look. Mimi walks out.
Jesus, I need a break bad!

Mimi comes back in pushing a rack full of assorted coats.

JUANITA
Hey! What's that you're pushin'? We're only workin' half a day!

MIMI
Addresses everyone.
These are the . . . uh . . . assorted styles.

JUANITA
Oh-oh. I bet you that rack is full of those heavy cheap coats.

OLGA
N'yet. Heavy coats — ve make-et noting-k monye.

GOLDIE
Mimi! Are there any more of the Elites in there, at least?

MIMI
Starting to distribute the coats.
You'll see what we have here. Just work and it will be fine.

JUANITA
Going directly over to the rack and quickly examining the coats, moans.
Oh, man, these are mostly the budgets.

MIMI
If you work fast, you will finish plenty!

JUANITA
Oh, sure — but how much money will we make?

MIMI
Moving the rack.
Some of them are budget and some are the more expensive line.

GOLDIE

Mimi! I want first choice this time! They all push in before me, and they get the best coats. Then I'm behind, and he yells at me.

MIMI

Hold your horses there. I'm in charge, ah?

JUANITA

Yeah, well if you're in charge, how come you didn't hand out those cheapos earlier? It's 'cause old Davis wants to lay 'em on us right at the end when we ain't got time to argue.

MIMI

You hold your mouth there about Morton.

JUANITA

He's 'Mr. Davis' to you, girl. You heard him. 'Morton'! La-de-da. Ain't we friendly?

MIMI

Choking back a response.

Take one coat at a time now.

Goldie rushes up first to select her coat.

GOLDIE

I'm taking first.

OLGA

Ven I take-et? Dis crazy, Golda, take-et all-a-time everyting before everybody.

GOLDIE

I was in this factory before you came to this country, you. I get first choice, that's all.

MIMI

Eh, eh. That is enough, ah? . . . I said you take one coat at a time. It all pays you money, ah?

49

JUANITA

Oh, yeah . . . sure! Ya just gotta work twice as hard for the same danmed buck.

GOLDIE
Walking back to her seat with a coat.

Ya . . . It's about time I got a good coat.

JUANITA

Ah, stuff it, Goldie! Just take the damned thing and sit on it. Olga, go ahead.
Olga, Sarah, and Huguette have taken their first coats and are at their work tables. Juanita is on her way to the rack.

MIMI

Okay. Take one at a time there like I told you, ah?
Walks out.

JUANITA
Looks sourly at Mimi.

Ah, can the 'like I told you'. You ain't told us nothin'!
In a lower voice.

He makes all the moves back there, and you just jump!
Olga, Sarah, and Huguette are sewing. Juanita is just starting to sew.

GOLDIE
Gets up suddenly and goes to rack muttering.

I'm just gonna take my second one near my chair. Just to be sure.

OLGA

Nefer mind-t. You not take now näder goot coat!

GOLDIE

Why not? I don't want to fall behind.

OLGA
Standing up.

N'yet!

Running back to the rack.

If you take-et two, I take-et two! I not sh-tupid!

JUANITA

Hey . . . hold it! Let's just do this fair and square this time!

GOLDIE

Well . . . that Olga is so big — she just pushes in and takes the best ones! I should take my two first to be sure I get good ones.

JUANITA

Why the hell should you get the first two? C'mon, lemme hear you!

GOLDIE

Well, at least that dummie Huguette should be the last one to take hers.

Pauses.

And Sarah, too, maybe!

JUANITA

What are ya? Nuts? You becomin' the boss-lady or somethin'?

OLGA

I vant now for sure to go before Golda! She not boss!

GOLDIE

Standing up.

Over my dead body! You won't go before me. I was here before any of you. Twenty-one years I'm here . . . I pick first.

OLGA

You go better to crazy house maybe. Cuckoo in head-t!

Sarah and Huguette are at their seats. They are the only ones who are seated while the women battle. Huguette fumbles with her coat, and Sarah — watching the screaming women — tries to quieten them down.

SARAH
Sh — sh. Shah. Let be already.
Mr. Davis comes into the work room.

GOLDIE
You mind your own business, you!

OLGA
Ah, shut up, you crazy.

JUANITA
Ain't nobody gonna be bossin' me, girl!

DAVIS
Okay, now what? Can't you do the job without arguing?

GOLDIE
I never argue, Mr. Davis. They start. They take my work away from me.

DAVIS
Look, you'll never get finished! You're wasting time! I don't care who does what as long as it gets done!

JUANITA
Yeah, but they're all different prices, Mr. D., so we gotta divide them even.

DAVIS
Mimi! Come here. I asked you to distribute these coats.

MIMI
But I explained everything to them.

DAVIS
Okay, I'll tell you exactly what to do, Mimi. Maybe you can do it then.

With exaggerated patience and deliberate over-simplification.
Divide those expensive samples evenly — see. Just count them, and divide them.
Mockingly.
Quite simple.

MIMI
But I have work in the office, Morton.

DAVIS
After that you can go back to the office and do your office work. The women can take the budget styles by themselves — because those are all the same prices . . . Okay?

MIMI
Okay.

DAVIS
Alright. Now I'll get back to the front room. And please, ladies. Everything has to be finished by one.
He exits quickly.

JUANITA
Hey, Mr. Davis! . . .

MIMI
Distributing the better coats from the second lot.
No more arguments today, ah? We expect you to finish the work in time.
Completing the distributing, she hands the last coat to Sarah.
Voilà, Sarah. Okay, now. *Vite, vite, vite.*
The women begin to work.

JUANITA
Hey, Mimi! We didn't get our break yet.

MIMI
Mister Davis said the break will be later today.

JUANITA
Yeah, well how about now? Ask 'im.

MIMI
I will speak to him soon.
Mimi exits.

JUANITA
Sewing, mumbles to herself, mimicking Davis.
'I don't care who does what . . .' Of course, he don't care who does what . . . He's just into making his big bucks . . . Damn!
The women are working silently and tensely now.

SARAH
So. At least he's a gentlemen. He divided, like, even for everybody.

JUANITA
Oh, hell, Sarah! He's no gentleman. He shouldn't be workin' us so hard!

SARAH
I don't know . . . he maybe needs everything before the Christmas vacation.

JUANITA
Yeah,well, we're gonna have to kill ourselves before we get to that Christmas vacation. And in the slack season, we sit around twiddling our thumbs. We either dead in here — or else we're killin' ourselves!

HUGUETTE
We soon go for the rest, ah? I will eat a piece of orange.

GOLDIE
Uch! Don't peel oranges today, Huguette . . . Yesterday your orange stank up the whole room!

HUGUETTE
Ben, dat's not bad smell, *des fruits*. I 'av to eat too, me.

SARAH
You'll eat, you'll eat, Huguette . . . Never mind Golde.

GOLDIE
I'm so thirsty, I'd like to sneak a drink of tea from my thermos.
Thinking out loud.
Oh, but what do I do if he comes in? He'll scream that I'm not working fast enough on his rush job here.

JUANITA
He sure is doin' a lot of rushin'. Only we're the ones runnin'!

GOLDIE
And what if I spill tea on one of his coats? So then, I'd have to kill myself already. Never mind. I'll wait for the break.

OLGA
Sighing.
I take-et lettle beet walk on break. You come too, Sarooshke?

SARAH
Sure, Olga. Why not? You're tired, Huguette?

HUGUETTE
Ben oui, j'suis ben fatiguée.

SARAH
Sure . . . Now it's already no joke.
Sighs.
But still, soon soon, it'll be finished the morning. You finish a day's work here, you go home tired,

you're glad already to see your house, and you feel also like a person which works.

HUGUETTE
Me, I 'av to take care of my boys at night. I make with them *les devoirs. Puis on mange tout ensemble.*

SARAH
You're a good mother, Huguette, the best. I used to sit also with my David, God bless him.

HUGUETTE
I read to my kids before dey go to sleep. Dey like dat.

SARAH
You'll see, Huguette. They'll come out by you very good boys.

Davis re-enters the room.

JUANITA
Well, here comes the man!

DAVIS
So, ladies. Coats running smoothly? Good, good, keep it up.

JUANITA
Mr. D.! Listen . . .

Davis is moving about and checking finished coats.

DAVIS
Keep moving, ladies. Good steady work today.

JUANITA
Hey, Mr. D. What about our break?

DAVIS
There's an awful lot to finish by one o'clock.

JUANITA
Yeah, well how about ten minutes now.

OLGA
Starting to get up.
Yah, yah! Sarooshka, ve make it now rest!

DAVIS
No! No! Hold on! Just run through those coats . . .
and you'll be all through by one.

JUANITA
Wha-a-t? That happened yesterday! We can't just
keep goin' . . .

DAVIS
Today is special. We have our Christmas celebration
at one.

OLGA
Ve need-et rest! Ees not matter Christmas.

GOLDIE
I want to drink some of my tea at least.

DAVIS
Now, look let's be good sports about this, eh?

JUANITA
Hell! How sporty do you want us to be, man?

DAVIS
Look, let's not hold this work off any more! Now, I
know I can count on you to get through this, ladies.
Just keep at it!
He exits quickly.

JUANITA
That man has got his nerve!
*She drags a finished coat back to the rack, delib-
erately dragging it on the floor as she walks.*
Jesus Christ! I'd like to step all over this damn thing,
I swear.

SARAH
In a loud whisper.

Juanita! Juanita. Don't pull the coat on the floor. Oi, he's watching there from the door . . . Pick up, dear.

JUANITA
Quickly lifts the coat off the ground, and continues to walk to the rack, carrying it with her.
Yeah . . .

HUGUETTE
Moi, j'suis bien fatiguée.

GOLDIE
Running back from the cooler.
I can't wait already till one o'clock.

JUANITA
I'll be dead by one o'clock!

SARAH
Sewing.
God forbid! Wait, dear. It'll soon be finished the morning.
Sighs heavily.

JUANITA
It's hotter than hell in here. Damn! Where's my bloody scissors now?
They all continue to work.

OLGA
Terrible! Tsk! Could have-et here heart attack!

SARAH
Oi, God forbid . . .
Lights dim to indicate the passage of time. Then lights rise again on the women hurriedly putting the last of the coats away, and beginning preparations for the Christmas party. Juanita pulls aside work chairs and footstools. Huguette and Goldie are clearing the centre of the room by pushing aside coat racks. Olga and Sarah carry

a long table to the centre of the room to serve as the main buffet or serving table. Mimi walks in and out carrying decorative pieces — crepe paper, a festive tablecloth, a stack of plates. . . As Mimi spreads the colourful cloth over the table, assisted by Huguette and Sarah, Juanita jumps up on a chair and begins to decorate the ceiling and walls with crepe paper and balloons.

JUANITA
Alright! We are going to get down! Hey, Goldie! Hand me some red paper!

GOLDIE
Uch . . . crepe paper and balloons. Such a big to-do.

JUANITA
Hey listen, you guys! We gotta start changing our clothes soon. Goldie, just hand me some more paper!

SARAH
Going into the bathroom to change.
So I'll go first. I'll be by you the first model.

GOLDIE
Awkwardly holding two rolls of crepe paper.
Red or pink?

JUANITA
Red and pink, baby! Red to match my dress and pink to match my cheeks. Yeah!
Goldie hands it to her.

HUGUETTE
Setting up plates and cups on table, giggles shyly.
It's same colour like my red dress.

JUANITA
Yeah, right . . . Matches you too, Huguette.

SARAH
Carrying her dress and shoes into the bathroom.
Oi, Huguette, you should maybe put on a smock for
now, so your dress will be fresh for the party.

JUANITA
Nah, nah, Sarah mama. We gonna freshen old
Huguette up with lots of fancy cologne and fine
make-up. Hand me some sparkles there, Goldie.

GOLDIE
What's with the big fuss? It's just a Christmas party!
I don't even want to stay.

JUANITA
You mean, you ain't stayin'? Oh, hey . . . that's too
bad. Just hand me some silver before you go, will
ya?

GOLDIE
Well . . . uh . . . I'm gonna stay. But . . . not for long.
Ten minutes I'll stay . . . Fifteen the most . . .

JUANITA
Uh . . . huh. Ten minutes, huh?

GOLDIE
Awkwardly.
Uh . . . there's gold paper. You want that too?

JUANITA
Yeah . . . right! We gonna make this sweat box shine.
We gettin' a one-week pass from this place.
Howls.
Whoee!

MIMI
At the table.
Bon, we will put a small decoration in the middle.
Pauses, taking another look at the table. Points.
Huguette . . . *tu va mettre les petites fleurs la-bas,*
okay?

*Huguette busies herself with the centrepiece,
and Mimi leaves the room. Sarah comes out of
the bathroom at this point. She is wearing a
navy dress, matching shoes, a strand of pearls
around her neck, and an antique brooch on her
collar.*

JUANITA
Whistles.
Hey, check that! Sarah, you look great!

SARAH
Nicer than the schmäte which we wear everyday,
eh?

OLGA
Yah, yah . . . Ees beautiful! Ah, you have-et leep-
stick, Sarah.

SARAH
So you see? Old can be also beautiful. A little colour
I put on the cheeks, a little bit lipstick, and I'm like
a new person. By my David, I'm already too old for
everything. A lot he knows.

HUGUETTE
Pointing to Sarah's brooch.
C'est beau, Sarah.

SARAH
Touching her brooch.
In the antique store, I bought. The older the
schmäte, the bigger the price! The pearls my husband gave me, may he rest in peace!

OLGA
If young-k man see you, ees make-et fall-een-love
right away.
Hums the wedding march.
Dai, dai, dai, dai.

SARAH
Laughing.
Sure, Olga, sure! From all sides they're running af-
ter me. A regular bride I am, eh?

OLGA
Laughs.

SARAH
Noo! . . . Go already, Olga! I want to see you in the
dress too. Golde, maybe you can go there together
to change.

OLGA
Yah, yah, Golda. Ve make-et together beautiful.

GOLDIE
It won't take me long.

JUANITA
Alright! Huguette, I need two more balloons up
here!
*Huguette hands her balloons. Sarah fusses with
the collar on Huguette's dress.*
There! That's it for the balloons!
Juanita gets off her chair.
Yup, okay, now . . . I'm gonna fix up Huguette's
make-up.
Pulls over a chair.
Sit down. We're gonna make you real pretty!
Sarah stands and watches.
HUGUETTE
Ben. I'm too shy for dat. Me, I don't put noting on
my face.

JUANITA
I ain't gonna put much on your face, honey. This is
Juanita's one second of sparkle job. Watch me
work!

Juanita brushes colour over Huguette's fore-
head and cheeks while Sarah watches.
This is the Juanita glow brush, girl! For party shine.
See that, Sarah?

SARAH
Oi, it's true. It makes like a nice finish all over, it's
true.

JUANITA
And now my magic blush, honey. Just highlights on
your cheeks.

SARAH
Oi, Huguette, it suits you very nice.

JUANITA
Uh-huh! Now this magic dew lipstick! Makes your
lips kissable.

HUGUETTE
I'm not can kiss nobody, me.
The three women laugh.

JUANITA
Quit laughin', girl. Let me line those lips first.

SARAH
Watching.
Oi! This makes such a beautiful shape!
Holding up a mirror.
Here, look Huguette. Wonderful, the red lips! A
beautiful face you have, altogether!

JUANITA
Stands back.
That's it. You're done, Huguette! And you look
pretty darned fine, I'm tellin' ya.

SARAH
Holding up a mirror for Huguette.
Beautiful, Huguette! Like a picture!

HUGUETTE
Pleased, looking at herself.
Ah, merci. My boys dey will be very happy to see
Mama *ce soir.*

SARAH
It will be by them a whole celebration when you
come in.

HUGUETTE
Oui, oui, Sarah.
*Mimi walks back into the room from the inner
office wearing a very chic dress.*

SARAH
Oi, look at Mimi! A wonderful dress. very elegant.
You changed by Mr. Davis in the office?

MIMI
Yes, Sarah. You like?

SARAH
Beautiful!

JUANITA
Abruptly.
I'm gonna get changed now. Hey, Goldie! Olga!
Come on out of there! I gotta get it on!
*Olga and Goldie come out, Goldie looking very
awkward and shy, almost girlish in a flowered
peasant skirt and ruffled blouse, and Olga
wearing a lavishly printed dress.*

JUANITA
Alright!

GOLDIE
Shy.
This outfit is nothing special. I have more.

SARAH
Nice, very nice, Golde.

Checks the material of Olga's dress.
Olga, you made yourself? Very good material.

OLGA
Yah, yah . . . I make-et myself.
Busies herself putting glasses out on the table.

SARAH
Rushes over to help her.
I'll help. Olgale.
Juanita goes into the washroom to change.

GOLDIE
Tugging at her skirt shyly, addresses Huguette.
So what are we supposed to do now?

HUGUETTE
We wait now for monsieur Davis, maybe.
They stand together.

HUGUETTE
It's look nice, the room ah, Goldie?

GOLDIE
I don't care about decorations.

HUGUETTE
You don't like to 'av a *fête*, you? You don't like dat
never?

GOLDIE
I don't know . . . maybe . . . sometimes. Uch . . . too
much of a fuss they make here. Such a . . .
*Juanita emerges from the bathroom now,
dressed in a sparkling red dress and high heeled
shoes.*

JUANITA
Here I come!

HUGUETTE
Ah, que tu es belle, Juanita.

JUANITA
Not bad, huh?

GOLDIE
It's nice. Very nice. You have a nice figure for that.

HUGUETTE
Eh, Sarah, Olga . . . come to see Juanita. *C'est pas mal joli!*
> *Sarah and Olga rush over. Huguette excitedly points to Mimi in the inner office at this point.*
Ah, Mimi, she look beautiful too.

JUANITA
She's havin' a thing with Mr. Davis. That's why she's all decked out. My dress is nicer though . . . It's all glitters . . . and I ain't dressin' for Davis either!

OLGA
Is true? She go vit Meester Davis? Yah, Sarah? E's make-et monkey business vit boss?

JUANITA
Hell, yeah . . . How else you think she got that cushy job?

OLGA
Yah, Sarooshka? Mimi go vit Meester Davis? Ees true?

SARAH
Who knows? Could be maybe . . . A good-looking man, Mr. Davis. I can't say no. A nice posture. Big shoulders. A young man inside; this I understand. A man sees fruit. . . he wants to taste. Who's to say?

OLGA
Sarooshka, ees not nice Mimi go vit married man! N'yet, e's . . .

SARAH
Who can know? My business? I have to sleep with
her at night?
The women all laugh together.

JUANITA
Hey, you're funny, Sarah!
*Mr. Davis comes into the room at this point,
and goes over to the table. The women, suddenly awkward in this social situation, seem to
freeze slightly. They huddle together at first.*

DAVIS
*Looking a little uncomfortable himself, begins
to pour wine into glasses, and smiles broadly.*
Come on, ladies. Come and have a glass of wine.
Help yourself.

SARAH
Goes toward the table.
Sure, a good idea! Coca cola you have, Mister
Davis?

DAVIS
Smiles.
Coke? Of course, Sarah.
Mimi approaches the table area.

MIMI
Come now, ladies, don't be shy.
*Puts her arm around Huguette, offers her a pa-
per plate.*
Viens, Huguette . . .
Hands a plate to Sarah.
Come here, Sarah. You must fill your plates and
make them happy, *non*. And drink your wine, ladies.
It's good for the blood, you know. *Voilà*, Goldie,
Olga . . . go take a drink.

SARAH

Come, come, Huguette. You have your health . . .
eat gezunte-reit! Olgale, come too . . . come with us!

OLGA

Ees very goot! Taste-et like halooshkes leetle bit,
yah!

SARAH

Smoke meat. Wonderful . . . Oi, Juanita. You shine
in that dress, dear. A regular picture!

JUANITA

Foxy, huh? That's me.
Turns around to show herself to Sarah again.
You know this dress cost me two weeks's pay — but
it's worth it! Hey, this wine's somethin'! You should
have some, Sarah!

SARAH
Giggling.
Me? Wine? No . . . Makes my head turn too fast.
You drink, dear. Where's Golde? Oi, good! She's
taking also a drink. Good.
She shouts towards Goldie.
Golde, come with us. Take a little bite, dear.

GOLDIE
Comes over hesitantly.
I'm not so hungry. I was thirsty before, that's all!

SARAH

Something a little bit to eat, Golde?

GOLDIE

I had breakfast. If I don't eat breakfast, I get a headache.

SARAH

So now eat lunch! It's already finished breakfast.
Take a näsh!

GOLDIE
I'll eat soon, maybe.

SARAH
Okay, good! Soon is good too.

JUANITA
We should have some kind o' sound in here! I hate to drink the wine without the music. Though the wine is real fine!

SARAH
Oi, music would really be a pleasure. Freilich.

DAVIS
Lifts his glass — speaks loudly.
Ladies, while you're relaxing, I want to congratulate you first of all on a job well done this morning. I knew I could count on you. And you did just fine!

JUANITA
Alright!
Lifts her glass.
For us!

SARAH
So I'll take already another little party sandwich to make a congratulations!

OLGA
Yah! I take-et too!

MIMI
And let's make a toast to Mister Davis, ladies. He's a jolly good fellow.

JUANITA
Snorts audibly.
Oops! Went down the wrong way that time.
Mimi comes over to Sarah and Olga, offering a plate of food. Juanita goes off to talk with Huguette and Goldie.

MIMI
You look very chic, Sarah.

OLGA
Yah, yah! Sarooshka look-et today like young-k lady.

MIMI
Ben oui. That's it, ah? Fresh as spring. You too, Olga.

SARAH
Oi! 'Fresh like spring', I like very much. In spring begins everything new. So we look like two young flowers, Olga. Wonderful.

OLGA
Drinking.
Yah. Dees you tell your David.

SARAH
Oi, a good idea. I'll tell him. Davidel! In the factory they tell me I'm like a fresh young flower. Why? Because with my friends, I get plenty happy. And by you under the stairs, what will I be?

OLGA
Laughing.
Yah! By heem een house, ees be only old-t flower! Kaput!

MIMI
Who is David, Sarah? Is that your boy?

SARAH
Yes, yes, David is my son, God bless him. This is already a long story. So, Mimi, tell me, what do you do over the holidays?

JUANITA
Hey, Mimi, we're all gettin' sort o' high here, and I wouldn't mind some music.

MIMI

Oh yes, that's a good idea. Yes, some singing would be nice.

SARAH

Oi, Golde's having a good time. You see, Olga? A pleasure to look.
Mimi goes off to Mr. Davis's side.

OLGA

Yah. Ees schnapps make-et happy. I told-t you!

SARAH

Oi, look, Mister Davis is holding up the hand. Sh-sh. Shah. Let's hear.

DAVIS

Just a little break in the festivities, everyone.
Holds up brown envelopes.
Your annual Christmas bonus!

SARAH
Shouts out.
Oi! In the same little brown envelopes. Like the Main Street millionaires!

OLGA

Yah!
Puts her arm around Sarah.
You and-t me. Two young-k millionaires.

DAVIS
Holds up the envelopes.
I'll be handing them out to you now with my best wishes.
Davis begins to distribute the envelopes to the workers, shaking hands or greeting them as he does so.

OLGA
Taking her bonus from Davis, shakes his hand.
Yah! Yah! Ees very gentlemen, Meester Davis.

Lifting her glass.
Yah, Merry Christmas!
She gulps the rest of the wine down.

SARAH
Oi, take a little food with the wine, Olga, so it doesn't make your head dizzy.

OLGA
N'yet! Not vorry!
Others laugh with her.

SARAH
Accepting her bonus.
Oi, thank you very much, Mr. Davis. It's very nice from you.

DAVIS
My pleasure, Sarah.

HUGUETTE
Accepting her bonus.
Merci, monsieur Davis.
Shakes his hand shyly. Comes over to Sarah's side.
Ah, Sarah, now I go buy *des cadeaux* for my boys.
Davis continues to distribute envelopes.

JUANITA
Rushing over to the circle of women, holding up her bonus.
Alright! A little extra cash!

HUGUETTE
Giggling.
C'est ben fin, ça.
She drinks more.

SARAH
Sure. Chanukah money. You see, Juanita? I have, thank God. But the grandchildren like a little better if you have more. It's only natural. And to have your

72

own? Not to have to ask anyone? Such a feeling you can't buy already.

JUANITA
Yeah. You got it, Sarah.

SARAH
Goldele, come! Put away your present in your purse.

JUANITA
You should treat yourself with that over the holidays, Goldie. Hey, I'm gonna get us more drinks. Another coke for you, Sarah? And I'll get you more wine, Goldie.

GOLDIE
Oh, thank you, Juanita . . . Next time I'll go and get.

SARAH
Come, Huguette. Here's Mimi with the little cakes. Take a sweet for good luck.

MIMI
Holding out a platter.
Help yourself, ladies, and happy holiday.

SARAH
To you too, Mimi.

HUGUETTE
Joyeuses fêtes, Mimi.

MIMI
Bonne santé.
> The warmth in the room spreads as the wine takes its effect. The women are becoming visibly more relaxed, shouting greetings and eating and drinking. Goldie, withdrawn from the others at first, is beginning to join them and to show more visible signs of involvement as she drinks wine. Davis stays on the sidelines now,

officiating, refilling serving plates, smiling,
pleasant and cordial, but clearly superior. Mimi
continues to function as social hostess, circulat-
ing among the women, laughing, refilling
glasses with enthusiasm. She clinks glasses
loudly with Davis at one point, and smiles
broadly. Then to encourage the festive spirit,
Mimi initiates the singing of a popular French
folk song.
Eh, ladies. I am going to sing for you a very happy
song.

HUGUETTE
Chantons 'Alouette'!

JUANITA
Yeah . . . something we can get into!

MIMI
It is a song about the good wine. You sing with me,
ah? *She begins to sing.*
Chevaliers de la table ronde,
Goutons voir si le vin est bon.
Chevaliers de la table ronde,
Goutons voir si le vin est bon.
Now you sing with me, eh, for the good wine, every-
body!
Goutons voir: oui, oui, oui,
Goutons voir: non, non, non.
Goutons voir si le vin est bon
Goutons voir; oui, oui, oui,
Goutons voir; non, non, non.
Goutons voir si le vin est bon.
Come on everybody; hold up your glass! *Huguette,*
chantons! Sarah! Olga! Sing with me, eh?
Mimi holds up her glass.
Goutons voir si le vin est bon . . .

The women begin to join in, spiritedly bringing their glasses up. The song picks up in intensity, as Olga, loosened considerably by the wine, sings the loudest. Olga's voice drowns out all the others with her substitution of the word 'Yah, yah, yah' and 'N'yet, n'yet, n'yet' for the 'oui' and 'non' part, forming a strange and intoxicating chorus of Ukrainian and French refrain.

EVERYONE
Goutons voir; oui, oui, oui,
Goutons voir; non, non, non,
Goutons voir si le vin est bon.

OLGA
Lai, lai, lai, yah, yah, yah,
Lai, lai, lai, n'yet, n'yet, n'yet,
Lai, lai, lai . . .
    The song continues, a feverish wild mélange of voices and sounds.

MIMI
    Sings second verse.
S'il est bon, s'il est magnifique,
On boira jusqu'à son plaisir.
S'il est bon, s'il est magnifique,
On boira jusqu'à son plaisir.
    Repeats the verse and initiates the chorus.

EVERYONE
    Loudly.
Goutons voir, yah, yah, yah,
Goutons voir, n'yet, n'yet, n'yet
Goutons voir si le vin est bon
Goutons voir, yah, yah, yah,
Goutons voir, n'yet, n'yet, n'yet
Lai, lai, lai, dai, dai, dai, da da.
    The singing continues for quite some time.

SARAH
Shaking with laughter.
Oi, my side is already hurting! Oi, a comedy.
The voices quieten down. They continue to drink and to eat.

JUANITA
Oh, hey . . . I liked that! Live sound!

SARAH
Maybe Olga will sing for us now. Olgale, sing dear.
You have such a beautiful voice.

JUANITA
Yeah, start us off on somethin' mellow, Olga.

OLGA
Yah, ve sing-et goot song from old days, yah
Sarooshka?
She starts humming the chorus of 'Those Were the Days'. She claps her hands as she begins the chorus, initiating a distinct heavy, steady rhythm.
Darogoy dalnoya, da nochyu lunnuyu,
Dai, dai, dai dai . . .
The others, recognizing the tune, join in and continue with the English lyrics of the chorus. Everyone sings, Mr. Davis's voice blending with those of the women.
Those were the days, my friend,
Dai, dai, dai, dai, da . . .
The pace in this scene is swift, the atmosphere is intoxicating as everyone drunkenly joins in. Olga seems to lead the singing. Mr. Davis hums in a deep voice. Olga stomps her feet.

JUANITA
Snapping her fingers, shouts over the voices.
Go on, do it, sisters! Sing your song!

The revelry spreads, building in intensity as Juanita grabs Sarah and Huguette to form a circle, and soon everyone is dancing together, hands linked, as they continue to sing and hum the song. The circle dance continues until Mimi forces Mr. Davis into the centre of the circle and the others clap their hands and sing more loudly, still dancing around him. They all applaud and raise their voices in song as Mr. Davis pulls Goldie into the centre with him. Goldie, flustered at first, engages in a slightly embarrassed version of a folk dance in centre circle, lifting her legs and skirt very awkwardly. As the women continue to dance and sing and urge her on, Goldie's dancing becomes much more animated, spontaneous, and fluid. She is no longer so self-conscious. There is an almost audible sense of revelation on the part of the women.

JUANITA
Good dancin', Goldie! Do it, girl! Get into it!

OLGA
Yah! Yah! Dance-et more, Golda!
Olga begins a revival of the chorus. Mimi rushes into the circle, and takes Goldie's and Mr. Davis' hands in her own. As Mimi becomes openly seductive, whirling around Mr. Davis with sensual rhythm, Goldie follows. The women shout approval and clap, forming the background beat for Goldie's and Mimi's dance.

OLGA
Shouts.
Yah! Yah! Mimi dance-et like Russian lady. Golda! Golda! Goot . . . yah!
Mimi moves her shoulders and hips. Goldie follows Mimi's movements.

JUANITA
Hey, Goldie. Do it! Do it! Ya got the fever, girl!
You're gettin' the spirit!

SARAH
Oi, Goldele, a pleasure to watch!

OLGA
Yah, goot!
*Davis disengages himself and joins the outer cir-
cle. Goldie is about to withdraw as well. Mimi
pulls her back, and the two women continue to
dance alone.*

JUANITA
That's it! Do it without him! Do your thing in there!
*The clapping and singing and dancing go on un-
til Mimi, exhausted, slows down, and bows
with exaggerated grace. Goldie rushes out of the
circle quickly.*

MIMI
Eh, Goldie! You dance very well, *ma belle.*

JUANITA
Yeah . . . you got the music in you.

SARAH
A pleasure to watch, I'm telling you.

GOLDIE
Oh, it's nothing! I was just dancing in a circle, that's
all.

JUANITA
Hey, you were doin' some steppin'! You caught me
by surprise there!

GOLDIE
Embarrassed.

Oh, stop it already. It was just a joke like. I mean why are you making such a big deal? Such a big fuss over nothing.

JUANITA
Okay! Cool it! Whoee! That was good! I need a drink now.
As she goes to get a drink, her dress catches on the side of the table, and it rips loudly.
Shee-it!
Examines her dress.
Why the hell didn't anyone cover that part of the table, for Christ's sake? This dress cost me an arm and a leg!

SARAH
T-sk T-sk. Oi, maybe we can give a sew . . .

HUGUETTE
Ah, c'est dommage, ça.
Mr. Davis moves swiftly over to Juanita's side.

DAVIS
Putting his arm around her.
Well, now, Juanita, we won't let one little ripped seam spoil our celebration! I'll arrange to have that repaired for you, okay? Now, let me take the occasion to make a toast to our Juanita.
Lifts his glass.
Here's to a good worker and a good sport! The fastest hand in the land. Hah! Hah!
The women clap.

JUANITA
Yeah, alright. No sweat! It's just a seam.
Raises her glass.
Thanks for the toast, you guys. And the same to you, everyone.

MIMI
And what about little Mimi, Morton?

DAVIS
Of course! Let's toast this wonderful party and express our special thanks to Mimi, our wonderful hostess today.
All raise their glasses.

MIMI
Olé. Mimi, that's me!

JUANITA
Okay! To a good party!

SARAH
Very nice! I make now a wish for a happy New Year and good health for everybody. With Coca-Cola, I make a very good wish, believe me.
All laugh and applaud. Mr. Davis holds up his hand, clears his throat, and the group quietens down to listen.

SARAH
Sh-sh. Let's hear.

DAVIS
I'll make this a short talk, everybody, so that you can go back to the party and continue to celebrate. Let me say first of all that you're a good working team. You're a fine-spirited group, and devoted workers. Without you our little factory couldn't operate. It's the word 'team' that's the most important to me. We start our day as a united team, and we end our day together as a united team. When we leave this factory at the end of each day, we do not leave it behind. No! We take it with us. It belongs in a real way to all of us. This factory doesn't belong to me. It doesn't belong to Olga. It doesn't belong to Sarah. No! This factory belongs to us, to all of us. We have

a common goal, ladies. We all strive to keep our little factory running smoothly. It means something to us, to each and everyone of us.

Pauses.

We don't just work together! We are all dedicated to the same cause. I want you to know that I appreciate that dedication. I want you to know that each of you is very special to me.

Lifts his glass.

So here's a toast to all of you . . . the people who work with their hands . . . the people who really care!

Brief applause.

I'll be heading home soon to join my family for the holiday, but I want you to stay as long as you like and continue to enjoy yourselves. The security man will close up when the last person leaves. Enjoy yourselves, ladies.

JUANITA
Alright! Let's have us another drink!

Davis leaves, waving good-bye, and Mimi prepares to leave with him.

MIMI
Okay, ladies. Have a good rest, eh? I take a lift with monsieur Davis. Merry Christmas!

As soon as they've walked out the door, Juanita lets out a wild howl.

JUANITA
Whoo-ee! Good riddance! What a lot of shit! Lordie, lordie, that man has got the corniest lines in the world!

She jumps up on a chair and imitates Davis, gesturing in exaggerated fashion, hamming it up.

JUANITA
This factory doesn't belong to me.

Hugs herself.

It doesn't belong to Olga.

Points.

It does not belong to Sarah!

Points.

No!

Emphatically. In a deep voice.

No . . . It's just all that there money that belongs to me.

Cracking an imaginary whip.

Work! Work! Work!

Holding out her hands and stuffing imaginary bills into her pockets.

Gimme! Gimme! Gimme!

The women laugh heartily.

JUANITA
Mimics again.

We don't leave this factory behind us. We take it with us.

Jumping down from her chair, she grabs Olga and croons.

Hey, Olga baby, just help me lift this little old factory, girl, so's I can carry it home with me. C'mon, let's just lift it up easy now. Let's show how much we really care!

Holds her heart melodramatically. She pants and squats, wrestling with the tremendous weight of the imaginary building. Pounds her breast.

I care! Don't you care, Olga!

OLGA
Laughing, crosses her heart.

Yah, Yah! I very much care. Yah! All-a-time, I carry factory een pocket. Hah!

JUANITA
What a lot of shit! Cracks me up!

OLGA
Yah . . . yah . . . ees talk-et like politicsman. Blah, blah, blah, blah. You make-et goot show, Juanita, yah!
Laughs.

HUGUETTE
'E talk like my cousin. 'E's priest, my cousin. 'E's make always big talk like dat.

JUANITA
That's right, Huguette. Come to Father Davis, and be saved, my lamb.

SARAH
Oi, Juanita. You're a smart girl and a regular actress. You're right. He has to make a speech so he throws together a few words. Like a decoration, that's all. Inside nothing!

OLGA
Blah, blah, blah.

SARAH
From the heart, for sure not. You want to hear from the heart, you have to listen to a friend, a family! Not to a boss!

GOLDIE
You know what was funny?
She starts giggling.
When you tore your dress there, Juanita, he got so scared, he thought you were gonna start a whole fight, like. He ran over so fast . . . I can't stop laughing . . . Did you see, Sarah? He was pale. And then he started to talk so fast from nerves! He's afraid of trouble.

JUANITA
Sings and snaps her fingers.
Yak-et-y-yak; blah, blah, blah, blah
Yak-et-y-yak; blah, blah, blah, blah
Yak-et-y-yak; blah, blah, blah, blah
That's all he does is
Yak-et-y-yak; blah, blah, blah, blah.
   They all laugh.
   Olga starts to sing 'Those Were the Days' hysterically.

OLGA
Dai, dai, dai, dai, da, da . . .

EVERYONE
Those were the days, my friend,
We thought they'd never end,
Dai, dai, dai, da, da . . .
   They all collapse with hysterical laughter.

OLGA
Breathless, drunkenly laughing.
Ve take-et now näder schnapps, yah?

JUANITA
Yeah . . . let's have a drink, and a real toast, none of that phoney shit. Hey, get your coke, Sarah! To a cool Christmas!

SARAH
A wonderful party!

GOLDIE
Yeah, it was very funny. I really laughed.

SARAH
   Oi, did you dance, Golde! Wonderful!

OLGA
Merry Chreestmas! Goot year! Yah!

HUGUETTE
Joyeux Noël!

OLGA
*Olga grabs Huguette and Sarah and waltzes
around the room with them wildly shouting.*
Merry Chreestmas! Goot Year!
Everyone laughs and shouts.
Merry Christmas!
*Giggles and laughter and tinkle of glasses
amidst shouts of joyous greetings...*
Goot Chreestmas! Yah! *Joyeuses fêtes*! Merry
Christmas! Alright! A Good Year, we should have!
Oi, a good year!
As lights fade.

Act Two

A week later. The garment factory. Goldie and Sarah are at their work-tables, Goldie is getting her materials for the day ready on the table. Sarah is sipping tea. The day's work has not yet begun.

SARAH

So, Golde . . . now begins a new year already. Oi, you danced so nice last week at the party.

GOLDIE

Ya, that was a nice party. Sure I danced. Why? You think I'm a wallflower or something?

SARAH

No, no . . . but t'was nice to see. Something a surprise by us. The party altogether was nice. My husband, may he rest in peace, used to say 'Happy occasions can never be too many.'

GOLDIE

Not like my father. Just the opposite. Uch . . . he hated a party. When I turned sixteen, I wanted a sweet sixteen party. Oh. Did he scream! 'A party? You're sixteen years old, you find yourself a husband. Never mind a party!' My mother brought me a cake and decorated the living room.

SARAH

So she made you the party anyways. Good. So what happened?

GOLDIE

So what happened? What always happened! He came into the house and he saw, so he started tearing the decorations and screaming. 'I work like a horse,' he screamed, 'and they're making parties on my money!'

Chuckles.

Oh, could he yell! 'Instead of making an arrangement with Myer to get herself a husband; they're making parties!' That's the way he used to talk.

SARAH

Oi, vey . . . Who was Myer?

GOLDIE

Oh, Myer worked in the butcher shop with my father. They were both from the old country. He was about forty years old, this Myer, and I was sixteen, so my father decided that I should marry him. Crazy, eh? I'm sixteen years old, a Canadian girl, and I have to marry an old butcher. My mother said, 'No! It's enough that I married a butcher,' she said. 'Goldie's gonna go to school yet. Never mind Myer.' My father could never forgive me and my mother that we said no. He...

SARAH

Tsk! Such a terrible story!

GOLDIE

I'm talking too much here already.

Laughs nostalgically as she begins to thread her needles.

That's another thing he used to say about my poor mother. 'All day she talks, she never closes her mouth!'

SARAH

Excuse me what I ask, but she's now okay, your mother?

GOLDIE

Not so okay! She died when I was nineteen. When she was alive, I worked in a small office part-time. My mother wanted me to work part-time, and to go to night school so I would become a somebody.

SARAH

It's true. To go to school is very important.

GOLDIE

But then, after she died, my father sent me to work full-time. He said that in a factory, you work fast, you can bring home a good pay. I remember when my mother was dying in the hospital, he brought her chocolates. It was the first time he did something like that. When she couldn't swallow anymore, he brought her chocolates.

SARAH

Sometimes we learn too late.

GOLDIE

And now, I cook for him and clean for him, and he doesn't talk about no Myer anymore.

SARAH

Oh, so you live with him? I didn't know.

GOLDIE

It's not such a big deal. He's eighty years old already.

SARAH

So you worked here the whole time, Golde?

GOLDIE

Ya. When I started here, Davis was a very young man. He wasn't even married then. He was nice to me too. We were two girls here. We used to work a lot of extra time. On Saturdays, he used to bring us coffee and lunch. He'd even bring us little presents. Once, I remember, he brought me a little bottle of perfume; another time he brought me embroidered hankies. He was just new in the business then.

HUGUETTE
Coming in, rushes over to the table.
Eh, Sarah, I 'av nice Christmas. My 'usband phone me. He talk to my boys. Dey were very happy. Maybe e's come back to me, *mon mari.*

GOLDIE
If you have money for him, he'll come back! They're all the same — men.

SARAH
It's good news, Huguette. With two boys, it's better with a husband than alone.
Juanita and Olga enter together.

OLGA
Ah, goot morning-k!

JUANITA
Jesus! It's late. Got us ten minutes to get going, Olga.

OLGA
Hanging up her coat.
Yah, yah!

JUANITA
How was your Christmas, Sarah?

SARAH
Very nice! I rested a little bit. My David came over with the little ones. But I was glad, already to come back today. It gets boring at home.

JUANITA
Sitting down at her place.
Hell! I wasn't bored! We partied on Christmas Day, on Boxing Day, on New Year's Day, and every day in between.

Mimi enters.

MIMI
Warmly.
Welcome back, ladies. Okay. Good. Mr. Davis will come in to tell you about the spring style. It's the new cape look.

JUANITA
Yeah, okay . . . I'll do any kind o' look: cape, tent, or blanket. I need the money!

MIMI
There will be plenty today. He's got a big order from the department store.

GOLDIE
He got an order from a department store? Imagine! He never had before from a department store, only from the small stores.

SARAH
Good, good . . . plenty work is plenty pleasure. Everyone will be happy.
Mr. Davis enters pushing a rack of coats.

DAVIS
Good morning. This is the beginning of the spring lot, ladies. It's a big order. There's the cape look for the petites, and the same cape look for the queen size this spring.

SARAH
Queen size?

JUANITA
He means over-size, Sarah. That's just a nice word for fat broads' styles.

GOLDIE
But one thing, Mr. Davis. The over-size should pay more. They take twice as long to finish.

DAVIS

Look here, Goldie. I don't want your complaints to-day. You always start a lot of trouble in here. I know all about that.

Goldie cowers.

JUANITA

Hey, but Goldie's right this time! The over-size should pay more. That's not fair to us . . . Not if you're doin' a whole lot o' queen-size business.

OLGA

Yah! In store, customer pay-et all a time more monye for over-size.

JUANITA

Yeah, that's right! You must make more on those, Mr. Davis. Why shouldn't we?

MIMI

It's true, Morton.

DAVIS

You stay out of this, Mimi.

Turns back to the women.

Look, we've been through this before. I'm sick and tired of going over it again.

Mimi goes off sheepishly to the office, comes back with a book and pen, and begins to work the rack, counting coats and recording details while Davis talks to the women.

JUANITA

Yeah, but that queen-size stuff is becomin' big business, Mr. D.

GOLDIE

Ya, that's true. I even saw some fat ladies modelling dresses on the television . . . for the 'full-bodied woman' or something.

DAVIS
That's enough! I don't need a run-down on the advertising business. You get paid for the coat, not for the size.

JUANITA
Yeah . . . well, we ain't happy!

DAVIS
You're not here to be happy, Juanita! This is a business I'm running. You want to work, or not?

JUANITA
I want to get paid right for my work, that's all I'm sayin'! I don't want to work for nothing.

GOLDIE
Me too. I don't want to work for nothing.

OLGA
Yah. Big coat, big monye.

DAVIS
Anyone else got complaints here?

SARAH
Timidly.
Maybe, Mr. Davis, we could have a meeting, come to make an agreement, so you'll be happy and we'll also be happy.

DAVIS
Look, I've had it with this talk. You're lucky you have jobs. Read the paper sometimes; you'll find out about unemployment.

GOLDIE
It's just not fair, that's all.

DAVIS
Well, you can go, Goldie. I can get along just fine without you. You're not the fastest worker in town . . . And you whine a lot.

Circling, stands in front of Huguette, deliberately towering over her.

What about you, Huguette? You have complaints too?

HUGUETTE
Non, monsieur Davis! Me, I'm not complain!

DAVIS
Alright then. You all had your chance to speak. Let's get moving.
Shouts.
Mimi!
Mimi comes over to his side.
You know what your job is. Do it, for God's sake! I don't want any complaints.

MIMI
Okay, okay.
Mimi busies herself, pushing small racks closer to each lady's table.

JUANITA
Shee-it! What a bastard!

MIMI
Quietly.
Okay, ladies. He's not in a good mood today, ah? Let's finish the over-size first.

JUANITA
Lugging a large coat to her table.
Man, there's about three coats in one here!

MIMI
Eh, Juanita! You will make fast money on the *petites* after. Settle down, ah.
Begins to distribute the petites.
Here, I will put the same number of petites for each worker, so you all have, for later.

93

JUANITA
Picking up her coat to start stitching.
Shit, this coat is huge! And the material, it's tough as leather!

OLGA
Starting to work on an over-size.
Aah, ees coat beeg for ten ladies.
They all begin to sew.

GOLDIE
Did you hear the way he yelled? Like I was nobody! You see? Huguette said she had no complaints! That's why we didn't get a better price for these over-size. Leave it to her to suck up to the boss.

JUANITA
Ah, cut it out, Goldie. It ain't her fault.

HUGUETTE
Ben, I don't know what to say, me. I'm scared to lose my job.

GOLDIE
Sure, you're scared. You spoil everything for us with your scared act there. You see, Juanita? We stick our necks out and she says no complaints. Did you hear him? 'I can do without you, Goldie.' Twenty-one years, and he can do without me!

JUANITA
Ah, we should just walk out!

GOLDIE
Ya, sure . . . we walk out, and we lose our jobs. You heard what he said! If Hugette would of at least complained too, we would get a raise.

HUGUETTE
But I'm just short time here. I don't have even my *chômage*, me.

GOLDIE

Sure, a good excuse! A short time you're here. So I'm here twenty-one years, and look what he said to me, eh? I could get scared too, eh? You collect a little bit from the church, a little bit from the children's help there, a little bit from charity, and God knows where. So why should you care for us?

SARAH

Oi, Golde, leave alone already. It's true. Two months Huguette works here . . . What can she say?

GOLDIE

Sure, sure! I know her type. Her type plays dumb. She lets him scream at me better.

SARAH

Oi, Golde, you're not talking right. Shah!

JUANITA

I'd just like to get my walking boots on! That's what I'd like to do.

OLGA

No, no . . . If you go-et out door, maybe lose right away job. Ees many peoples now not vork!

SARAH

So shoin! Let's already work here.

JUANITA

Hey, I'm almost out of the round black buttons for these. Got some extra there, Goldie?

GOLDIE

Ya . . . Here.

Hands buttons to Juanita.

But remember, Huguette really spoiled it for us today. It's her fault.

Goes back to her seat.

Hey, Huguette, why don't you carry the rest of the heavy coats over to our tables today? Why should I get a hernia? After twenty-one years, I should carry? I carried plenty. He thanks me very nice. You carry today.

JUANITA
Ah, lighten up, Goldie!

GOLDIE
Never mind! If she would have said something, we would be getting fifty cents more for each coat. You could pay your bank loan, there, Juanita . . . easy . . . with fifty cents more a coat!

JUANITA
Ah . . . cool down, Goldie.

GOLDIE
Never mind 'cool down'. Huguette should carry the coats! You got no complaints, eh Huguette? So you carry.

SARAH
Leave alone, Golde! What are you making a business from the wrong person?
Quietly.
Maybe we could talk to him tomorrow about a better price. After all, this is a union shop.

JUANITA
I ain't goin' to no union, I'll tell you that.

SARAH
I mean, we'll talk to him first quietly-like . . . so he'll make with us an agreement here maybe.

GOLDIE
And what if he doesn't agree?
All the women are silent.

SARAH

So . . . uh . . . if he doesn't agree . . . So . . . it's maybe trouble. But he'll agree, he'll agree; it's a union shop.

JUANITA

Ah, hell! I don't trust that union shit anyways. That's why I've never gone to them since I'm here. Those union people are the same as the bosses. Fat cats!

SARAH

No, the union is for the workers, Juanita. My husband used to know about the union.

JUANITA

I went to those union guys once at my last job about a longer lunch break, and the man talked my ear off . . . I mean he talked real pretty like, but that's it. And then, the boss was on my tail for weeks! It got so bad, I had to quit, and the union didn't do nothing for me then!

OLGA

Yah! Mine husband vork in union shop. They make-et complaint. Ees right away make-et strike, dis union!

Scoffs.

Ah! Seet een house! Ees get after ten cents raise! Not goot! I tell-et.

GOLDIE

That's right. When they vote for a strike there, even if you don't want, you have to stop. You can lose two months work! For a ten cent raise! And Juanita's right! If Davis ever knew that one of us went to complain, we'd have to quit already.

SARAH

So you never went to the union, Golde? In twenty-one years?

GOLDIE

No, I never went. We had a strike once, but some workers in another factory started it, so he couldn't start up with me.

JUANITA

Ah, hell . . . let's just work! Just talkin' about the union is makin' me sick!

OLGA

Can break-et finger, so hard-t coat!

JUANITA

Hell! I should just go on welfare.

Chuckles.

That's a real cat and mouse game, though. My girlfriend was on it. First, you gotta fill out a whole lot of forms and, then, answer dumb questions. 'Do you have a consort?' They don't talk plain English, those folks, you know? 'Do you have any dependants?' 'Any property?' Hell, they want to know everything about you! They got them big computers and they got your whole life clicked into them. Shee-it!

OLGA

Not understanding Juanita's references.

Yah, yah . . . Mine Alex know-et everything from computer machine.

JUANITA

And here's the best part! They keep checkin' you out so you're not livin' with anyone, you know? That's what they did with my girlfriend. They drove her crazy. Got to hide your man in the cupboard or somethin' when they come round to check you out!

Laughs.

And you know what they're payin' now for a single person under thirty? Nothin! Not enough to buy your toilet paper!

SARAH

I know already from the pension that they're not such big givers.

GOLDIE

I wouldn't take welfare anyways. I never took charity.

JUANITA
Getting up to take another over-size.
Hell . . . these fat-broad styles are beginning to feel alright when you start thinkin' of what you gotta go through to get welfare.
Snaps her fingers.
Let's make that music louder, and work!

GOLDIE

Wait a minute. Huguette! Carry that coat for Juanita. And bring me another one here too.

HUGUETTE

Ben, I'm not carry for everybody. Me too, I work here!

GOLDIE

You can carry. You had no complaints, so carry!

JUANITA

Hey, don't get so bitchy, Goldie. I can carry my own coat!

SARAH

Golde! Golde! Stop! What do you have to her? You made a complaint, so did it help? This is not the right way to make a complaint anyways. The right way is to go all together and talk like a person with him.

GOLDIE
Shrilly.

You know something, Sarah? You make me sick too!
Always with your sweet little ideas.

Mimics Sarah.

'Let's make a meeting, Mr. Davis, and an agreement,
Mr. Davis — so you'll be happy and we'll be happy.'

Scoffs.

You make me sick!

SARAH
Angry.

I'm not so much excited from you too, Golde. Anyways, I know what I'm talking. My husband used to
be the shop chairman for his place. And they used
to go always to the union to make a complaint and
come to an agreement. And before that when I
worked on Main Street, we went together to the
boss to complain and the boss had to agree to a better price, because it was the busy season and he
couldn't let go in the middle of the season eight
workers.

Almost shouting.

So I'm not so stupid, Golde! I know what I'm talking. You hear? Because I'm older I don't know already anything!

GOLDIE
Oh, you and your husband and your Main Street!
What do you know? You're talking about a hundred
years ago, there!

SARAH
What do I know? What I already forgot, Golde, you
maybe will never know!

GOLDIE
Oh . . . I wish you'd forget to talk so much!

OLGA

Ach, Sarooshka . . . you not listen to Golda!

SARAH

You hear, Olga? She danced at the party, so I thought maybe it's something a change. But nothing. Golde is Golde! Feh! A shame!

Mimi comes in.

MIMI

Okay, ladies. How is the work going?

JUANITA

It's goin' real slow. No kiddin', these coats should really pay more.

MIMI

Well, it's up to the boss.

JUANITA

Well . . . talk some reason to him.

OLGA

Yah, you tell-et heem!

MIMI

I can't tell him what to do. He's my boss too. Anyways, you take a short break now. Maybe that will help, ah?

Mimi exits.

JUANITA

Yeah . . . I'm going to the stand for a coke.

SARAH

So, Huguette, how went the last coat?

HUGUETTE

The last one, it was not so 'ard like before.

SARAH

Laughs.

Yes, sure, you mean you got used to your troubles.

HUGUETTE
I go now take some water.

SARAH
So, Golde, you're getting used to your troubles?

GOLDIE
Drinking out of her thermos cup and standing up.
It's not so funny.

SARAH
But it's not so serious also. It's a joke. Even with serious things is sometimes funny too.

GOLDIE
Okay, okay. So it's funny maybe.
The women relax for a few minutes. Juanita comes back into the room. Goldie rushes off to the bathroom.
I'm going to the bathroom now, 'cause after, we won't get a chance. Don't touch my things.

SARAH
Huguette, take a little bit tea from me, dear.

HUGUETTE
Non, merci . . . I drink water.

OLGA
Yah, I now fast drink tea.

GOLDIE
Running back from the bathroom.
Is she coming back already or what?

JUANITA
Don't sweat it. She'll be here.

MIMI
Enters.
He's coming in to have a look. Now, ladies . . .

The women start to busy themselves at their seats. Davis enters. Mimi stands by.

DAVIS
Walks around the room.
So how's the work going in here?

OLGA
Ees too hard-t!

DAVIS
Keep at it, ladies. It's good practice!

JUANITA
Mutters.
What are we practicin' for — the Olympics?

DAVIS
Let's see how many you finished here?
He checks the racks.
Oh, oh . . . wait a minute. These aren't moving fast enough. Juanita, I'm disappointed in you. You're not getting enough done, here. I thought you were one of my fastest workers.

JUANITA
Well . . . hell, I did the best I could before the break.

DAVIS
Break? What break? Mimi! Who told you to give them a break so early?

MIMI
Ben, they were very tired. I thought you . . .

DAVIS
You don't think nothing! You ask me before you make a decision! A break this early is stupid!

MIMI
But you told me to give the ladies a break when they need one. And they needed one now, I could see.

DAVIS

I am dealing with a rush job here! And so I'll tell you what's needed.

MIMI

Well, okay . . .

DAVIS

I'll lose my season in here. They work like turtles — and you make all the wrong moves. You're quite a team I got myself . . . Now look, Juanita, if this is your best work, maybe your best just isn't good enough for me. I'm competing for business out there, you understand? I've got to deliver the goods on time! You . . .

Mimi exits to office quickly.

JUANITA

Well, geez, I only got two hands.

DAVIS

Maybe I need faster hands. You keep that in mind.

He goes over to look at Goldie's coats. He nods his head disapprovingly.

This is bad, very bad. Can't see why you're doing all that complaining. You, of all people. You're getting kind of slow. Sloppier all the time too.

GOLDIE

Frightened, her voice trembling.

But this cape style is even harder to finish than the normal over-size. I can't go any faster.

DAVIS

The cape look is what I'm delivering. Now you're telling me you work only on styles that you like?

Goldie cowers.

Okay, okay. I know what's going wrong in here. You're talking too much instead of concentrating on the work. No, no. This won't do! It isn't Christmas

104

anymore. I want speed! No excuses! Let's have some production. And tidy up the work there, Goldie. Mimi! Come back in here, will you?

Mimi comes back into the room.

This work is not going fast enough for me. You're supposed to set the ground rules in here. Now you better make sure you do it!

He exits.

MIMI
Moves into the centre of the room.
Okay, ladies . . . don't worry.

JUANITA
Almost in tears.
He's treating us like dirt.

MIMI
You just finish these and you'll be okay. It's a new customer, you know. It makes him nervous.

JUANITA
Jesus, I don't know if I can take anymore of his nerves.

Mimi exits.

GOLDIE
Speaks in choked voice.
You know why he picks on us, Juanita? Cause they don't talk.

OLGA
Vat you vant? I tell-et heem, no?

GOLDIE
Sure . . . you told him, but the other two . . . nothing! Hey, Huguette! Why don't you help us out today, eh? Leave your petites for us, and you do only the big ones, okay?

HUGUETTE

Only big coats for me? *Ben non, c'est pas fin, ça.*

GOLDIE

It's 'fin', it's 'fin' enough. You're new here, right? So it's the way it should be.

SARAH
Adamantly.

No, this I won't let! This is for sure not right.

GOLDIE

Ah, shut up, Sarah. You're always acting like a goodie-goodie in here. 'This is not right, that's not fair.' Don't worry about her! She has more money than you. She collects from everywhere, I bet. The French know how.

MIMI
Coming in to distribute more thread, overhears Goldie.

Eh, you don't talk before me like that, Goldie, ah?

GOLDIE

I don't mean you, Mimi! I mean her kind, from the low class.

MIMI
Very angry.

Merde! Don't give me that bullshit. Ah! You're crazy! You sleep with your coats, that's why.
She spits her words out.
No more *maudit* bullshit from you!
The office phone rings and Mimi exits to answer it.

GOLDIE
Goes to the big rack.

Hey, Juanita, come over here a second.

JUANITA

Ah, leave me alone. I'm feelin' mean now!

106

GOLDIE

No, no . . . I just want to show you something! It's important.

JUANITA

What the hell do you want?

GOLDIE

Just come over, Juanita, for a second.

JUANITA

Going reluctantly over to Goldie.

Oh shit, this better be fast! I gotta keep workin'! He's really on my tail today.

OLGA

Ah, ees make me crazy dis coat!

Goldie and Juanita speak to each other near the big rack.

GOLDIE

Look, Juanita, he's starting up mostly with us, right? And we're gonna be in trouble. If Huguette would do only over-size today and no petites, we could work much faster. I'm telling you, it's only fair.

JUANITA

Ah, can it, Goldie! That ain't fair at all!

Starts to move off.

GOLDIE

Look, you want to know something? He doesn't scream at Huguette 'cause she's French, like Mimi. He screams mostly at me and you, right? And you know, Mimi talks to Huguette in French all the time . . . who knows what they're saying? I mean the French stick together. I bet they laugh at you together. Look, Juanita, Huguette isn't really entitled to the same as us. She just came here two months ago. It's not like we're not letting her work. We're

107

just asking for a chance to get more of the small sizes, so he won't keep picking on us so much.

JUANITA

Ah, look! Stop buggin' me. I don't play dirty like that.

Takes another coat and walks back to her seat.

GOLDIE

Walking back to her chair with another heavy coat.

Okay, okay, Juanita. Some people just get fooled all the time. That's why he talks to you like you're a nobody. He never talks to Mimi like that. Not like that!

JUANITA

Shut your face, Goldie!

OLGA

Sewing.

Vat you talk-et there sh-ecret, Golda?

GOLDIE

It's no secret. Anyone can hear. I'm just saying that Huguette should do the big coats today and leave the petites for us. That's all. Look at that, Olga. You're here four years, eh, and Huguette gets the same work as you. Is that fair? Just 'cause she's French, like Mimi, and you're not?

OLGA

Ah, vat you talk-et? I must vork fast. Boss soon come back, make-et scream here! I need now big scissor.

She gets up to get the large scissors from a side table.

GOLDIE

If you'd listen to me, you wouldn't have to worry about him screaming. If she was only decent, she'd do the big coats today, and give us a chance.

SARAH
Golde! Golde! You're even meaner than I thought!
How could you expect one woman to do only over-
size?

HUGUETTE
C'est pas juste, ça.

GOLDIE
It's joost, it's joost! You had no complaints, so it's
joost!

HUGUETTE
Eh, I'm not can do only over-size, me.

GOLDIE
Why not? 'Cause you have a special arrangement in
French there with Mimi?

HUGUETTE
Angry, her voice shaking.
Ben, it's nothing bad to talk French, eh? What you
want, you? Mimi, she's *ben gentil.*

GOLDIE
Oh ya? She's your friend, eh? You hear that,
Juanita?
Juanita does not respond.

HUGUETTE
She's good lady, Mimi! She's my friend, sure!

GOLDIE
See what I mean Juanita? They're like this.
Crosses her fingers.
Special friends, special favours. I'm telling you,
she's not so quiet, this one. She's smarter than all of
us with her little tricks.

OLGA
Juanita, you have-et brown cotton?
Mimi enters.

109

MIMI
Is it okay in here, ladies?

JUANITA
We need some brown thread.
Mimi starts going off to the supply table for re-fills. Davis comes in again.

DAVIS
Walking around the racks.
Speed picking up in here, Mimi?
Stops to look a little more closely at the coat which Juanita is working on.
Wait a minute! You have to use the thick cotton for this lot, not the regulars. Mimi! How come this one's using the regular cotton here?

MIMI
Well, I didn't notice that Juanita was . . .

DAVIS
Well, it's your job to notice! What is it with you? Where's your head? I can't believe this! Whatever happens in here is your responsibility! You got that?
Indicates Juanita.
Ger her to rip that coat up — and make sure that none of the others are using the regular on these heavy coats. I don't want to see anymore mistakes in here!
Davis storms out.

MIMI
Eh Juanita! Eh, eh . . . it's easy to see that this material is too heavy for the regular cotton, ah?

JUANITA
Well, shit! I didn't know . . .
Plaintively.
I been usin' it on all my black coats. Nobody told me.

110

MIMI

Oh, non! Qu'est-ce qui se passe? Eh, you don't have to be a genius to know that.

JUANITA

Well, what the hell am I going to do now?

MIMI

Ben, okay . . . Maybe they'll pass, ah? Just keep your mouth closed, ah? But pay attention. Do I have to check on you like a baby every five minutes? Look here, everybody. We have to go faster in here, ah? No more fooling around. You heard Mr. Davis, ah?
She gets the thick brown cotton from the side table now and hands it to Juanita.
Here, Juanita. Rip that coat up there, and start over.
Bitingly.
It's the thick for the heavy coats and the thin for the thin. Eh, use your brain there . . .
Mimi exits.

JUANITA

That bitch! Lordin' it over me again.

GOLDIE

Humph! Now she's acting like your boss. Just 'cause you forgot the heavy cotton. Actually, Juanita, you should have her job. You've been here just as long as her.

JUANITA

Back off! I'm in enough of a sweat!

GOLDIE
Sewing.

Who's on your back? I'm only saying what's true. Me, I'm not young enough for that job. But you're her age, and you're just as pretty. You think you couldn't work a little in the front office like her, and then hand out the work in here? You could do it. It's

111

'cause she's French like this one, and she fights for her rights. You gotta be tricky to get ahead in this world.

JUANITA
Don't hassle me, Goldie!
Gets up.
I'm going to get another coat.

OLGA
Getting up.
Me too. I go take-et.

GOLDIE
I don't care . . . I'm gonna do one more over-size after this, and then Huguette should work on those big sizes. It's us three who did more over-size than anybody today. We're working like horses!

SARAH
Golde! Golde!

GOLDIE
Never mind!
She rushes over to Huguette's coats on the rack.
Look here! Huguette finished only three of these big ones. She's smart. She'll finish only a few big coats today, and tomorrow, when we get small ones, she'll work very fast, and make up for it. At the end of the week, she'll make a much bigger pay than us.

OLGA
Suddenly angry.
Huguette! You no make-et tricks here! You feenish fast over-size. Same like us.

SARAH
Olga, please, stop!

HUGUETTE
Ben, me too. I work over-size. What you want? I'm not so fast like you.

112

GOLDIE
Goes back to her seat and sews.

Tomorrow, we'll be so tired from working so hard we won't have strength! And Huguette will do all the work on the small ones. Olga, your face is very red, you know. You could get a stroke or something. You get high blood pressure when you have to work so fast.

OLGA
Rushes over to the mirror on one side of the room and looks.

Vat you talk-et? Ees too-much red, mine face? Sarah, ees bad colour?

SARAH

Oi, Olga, it's a natural colour. It's hot in here. We're all red.

OLGA
Sitting down.

Yah, yah. I not sick. You leef me alone, Golda.

GOLDIE
Seductively.

Hey, Juanita, wouldn't you like a drink or something?

JUANITA

Waddya? Crazy? I ain't got time to drink now.

GOLDIE
Looking into the office.

Oh, look, Mimi's sitting on the desk now, and she's drinking a coke. Gee, Davis treats her like a queen. Not like us. She's smoking a cigarette too.

JUANITA

He don't treat her like no queen!
Speaks quickly.

Hey listen, I'm gettin' a migraine now. I can't keep up this speed anymore. After lunch, I want to do the petites, and Huguette can finish the rest of the big ones. Hell, there's not that many over-size left anyways.

SARAH
Oi, Juanita, please. You're starting too?

JUANITA
Hey listen, Sarah . . . Don't start playin' lawyer in here.
Aggressively.
Huguette does the rest of the big ones today. That's it. Them's the breaks! I got bills to pay, and I gotta look after myself! Think it's fair the way Davis is treatin' me?

SARAH
But we're talking now about Huguette, not about Mr. Davis.

JUANITA
Never mind that shit! I've had it! I'm tired of being a sucker! That's it! Huguette does the rest of them over-size.

GOLDIE
Smugly.
That's what I'm saying the whole time.

JUANITA
And listen, Goldie! Shut your face now! I'm sick of you!
Bursting with fury.
You got a real awful voice! You know that? You sound like a goddamned parrot!

GOLDIE
Oh, ya? Well at least a parrot can talk English the right way. I bet you didn't even finish high school.

JUANITA
You know somethin'? If it weren't for this goddamn
rush on these, I swear I'd get up and hit you in your
face! I just can't take the time out right now. You're
lucky!

SARAH
Oi, now already it's a boxing match by us! And I'm
in the middle. Smarter already to sit at home with a
glass of tea. And on top of that, you put all the work
on Huguette!

JUANITA
Sarah, stop that referee shit in here. I can do what I
want!

SARAH
But, Juanita. We're people who danced together,
and work together. Please . . . Everybody should
have the same number of petites. Please . . . not that
Huguette should do only the heavy coats.

HUGUETTE
Almost in tears.
Ben oui, Sarah. C'est pas juste du tout!

JUANITA
Hey look, Huguette, lots of things ain't fair in this
world. You're new here and you're cuttin' into our
territory! You gettin' work, ain't you?

SARAH
Olga, maybe you could understand. Say something!

OLGA
Ach, mine needle break-et een coat now! Leef me
alone.

HUGUETTE
Shouts in a breaking voice.
You don't make me work only big coats! I'm com-
plain to Mimi!

GOLDIE

Oh, you hear? You hear? She's gonna complain now
. . . You hear? To Mimi, yet! You don't listen when
I talk to you, Juanita, eh? Before, when she could
really help us with Davis, she said she couldn't complain 'cause she's here only two months, right? Oh,
she's a tricky one, I'm telling you.

JUANITA

Hey, Huguette! That complainin' to Mimi don't sit
right with me. I don't like the sound o' that.

GOLDIE

She probably always runs to Mimi . . . to tell everything . . . about all of us. And Mimi tells the boss!
That's why he's screaming at us today.
Calls out.
You see, Olga? Juanita understands already. They
have a secret there, her and Mimi. Cause they're
both French, they can talk secrets. She's like a spy in
here.

OLGA
Shouts.
Yä ti bi däm!
She gets up, shaking her fist at Huguette.
Vat you do-et? You make-et espionäge here? You
nefer mind-t complain! Only beeg coats, you make-
et now!

SARAH

No, Olga! I can't believe this! Please listen to me,
Olgale.

OLGA

N'yet! I not listen you. She make-et here sh-ecret
espionage.
Raising her fists to Huguette.
Yä ti bi däm!

116

GOLDIE
That's right. She's Mimi's little pet, I told you!

JUANITA
I ain't gonna work my butt off for a lousy tattle-tale!
You get last choice to pick tomorrow.

SARAH
Juanita! Please. For a coat you're breaking a person
altogether?

JUANITA
I don't care about the coat part. I don't like stoolies.
I don't like that 'complain to Mimi.'

HUGUETTE
Starts to cry.
I don't do noting bad, Sarah. I 'ave *mal à la tête* now
. . . I never do noting to dem.
Sarah comforts Huguette.

SARAH
Don't cry, Huguette. Don't cry. I'll help you with all
the big coats anyway. T-s-k! T-s-k! To make a person cry! Tomorrow already they'll maybe better understand.
*Helps Huguette adjust the coat on her lap. The
room is silent, and the women sew tensely.*
You know what my father used to say, Huguette? A
peasant in Europe can't open his mouth to the rich
landowner, so what does he do? He goes home, and
he beats up very good his wife! And the rich man,
when he hears about it, says 'So what can you expect
from a peasant?' So it goes like that! Do you know
what I mean, Huguette?

HUGUETTE
Crying.
I don't understand now, Sarah. I'm much nervous.

117

SARAH

Here, I'll better start for you this coat. Never mind now stories from my father. Another time. Shoin!

Tense silence for a short while.

GOLDIE

Juanita, how many did you finish already?

JUANITA

Enough! I'm almost ready for the smaller ones. Boy, can't wait for this lousy day to end!

GOLDIE

Oh! He'll yell at me for sure now! I can see from the rack I finished less than you. Who knows what he'll say to me now?

Huguette is heard sniffling loudly in the background.

Oh, listen to her crying in the middle of everything! I'm nervous, my hands are shaking. He's gonna yell who-needs-you-Goldie, and she's crying for my nerves!

Shouts.

Shut up, Huguette! What are you crying for? You want to make more money than the rest of us, so you can buy your husband back, maybe?

HUGUETTE

Letting out a loud cry of fury and pain, drops the coat she's working on, and rushes out of the room.

J'en peux pus! C'est assez!

The women look up, shocked. Sarah attempts to run after Huguette, and within a moment, the loud noise of a fall is heard outside the factory door. The three remaining women jump up and gasp.

JUANITA

What the hell!

118

OLGA
Vat is'?

GOLDIE
What happened?

SARAH
Is heard shouting outside the door.
Oi, Mimi! Call a doctor. Oi, Mr. Davis! Do something! She fell!
Movement is heard outside the door, sounds of consoling voices.

MIMI
Reste tranquille, Huguette.

DAVIS
Overlapping.
Mimi, make sure no one moves her. Easy there, easy Huguette. Just make sure nobody moves her! Tell her she'll be fine.

OLGA
Running to the door.
Ees accident?

GOLDIE
Running after her.
I think she fell! I didn't mean for her to fall, honest!

OLGA
Outside the door, a little hysterical.
Ah, ees make-et hurt! Juanita, you bring cold water for Huguette. Please! Juanita!

JUANITA
She paces inside the room.
Jesus, ain't that the end? I ain't even gonna look.

GOLDIE
Rushes back into the room, runs the tap, and starts out with water.

119

I'm bringing her cold water! Maybe we should put cold water on her face!

Juanita goes towards the door, then turns back into the room, disgusted and discouraged. She paces. There's a great deal of movement and noise outside.

JUANITA
Ah, hell! Now ain't that the pits! Everything turns to shit around here. It's always the same. Nothin' ever turns out right.

Sarah walks back into the room.

SARAH
Oi, it's hard already to look!

JUANITA
Is she hurt bad, Sarah?

SARAH
Oi, what's to talk?

She starts to cry.

My David's already right. This is not for me. Enough. I'm . . . too old . . . for this. I . . . can't already. It's . . . time.

JUANITA
Hovers over Sarah.
How bad is she hurt, Sarah?

Olga and Goldie come back into the room.

GOLDIE
He made us go back in. He told Mimi to go with her in the ambulance. How could she fall so hard? Maybe she tripped over a packing box.

OLGA
Ah-h, ees terrible! Ees danger-much fall on steps.

JUANITA
I knew something awful was goin' to happen sooner or later in here.

GOLDIE

Who expected such a thing!

OLGA

Yah! Een one meenute . . . ees happen terrible accident.

SARAH

'One minute,' she says . . . 'one minute.' It's not one minute, Olga! It's a whole morning you're pushing her and pulling her till she runs out already like a crazy person! She didn't fall for nothing.

Gulps back tears.

It's a shame what you did to her. From aggravation, she fell!

The women are silent. Juanita paces. Olga stands still. Goldie goes to the sink.

GOLDIE

I have to drink some water!

JUANITA

Sooner or later, the shit's gotta hit the fan somehow . . .

GOLDIE

What are we supposed to do now anyway? Wait for him?

SARAH

Maybe you should make together here a dance 'cause Huguette will be lying in hospital, and you'll have already all of her coats! A shame!

Her voice shaking with anger.

You, Olga! . . . In you I'm the most disappointed. To start a crazy business from an espionäge, all of a sudden, with a poor woman. I asked you, 'Olga don't start,' but no, you wouldn't listen!

OLGA

Vat you vant, Sarah? I not break-et Huguette's foot. Ees Golda make-et argument here. I not . . .

121

JUANITA

Yeah, you are one mean bitch, Goldie. You've been on her case all morning, working us all up, till we don't know what the hell we're doin' anymore!

OLGA

Yah . . . yah! You bädt lady, Golda. God veel make you something bädt, you! All the time fight for more monye! Vat you need-et so much monye, ah? You not have familye! You bädt lady!

SARAH
Standing up.

Never mind, Olga! It's by you very easy to blame one person. So Golde started, but you listened to her. You're the same like her! Don't think you fool me . . .

Frantically, she grabs her shopping bag and starts packing her personal belongings. Frenzied, she throws in a thermos bottle, scissors, thimbles . . . She drops the shopping bag, and runs off to the hanger, starts pulling her coat off of it, until the hanger jerks off completely and falls heavily onto the floor.

Enough!

She yanks her sweater sleeve down, trying to slip her arm into the coat.

It's enough for me!

She throws the coat down on a chair. She sits down, starts tugging at her boots. Pulls one on.

I can't stay here anymore. I'm going already home! Finished! You're the same like her Olga. Exactly the same. I don't need you for my friend altogether. Such . . . friends . . . I don't need.

She walks over to her table.

Finished! Enough with the factory! I'm going . . . home!

122

She looks around for her purse. Picking it up, she starts putting a few of her small personal things into it from the work- table. She picks up her coat.

OLGA

I not care, Sarah! You no like-et me, you go home! Nefer mind. All the time you make-et speech. Ees Golda start here trouble. Ees . . . crazy.

She spits on the ground at Goldie's feet.

GOLDIE

Sure, go ahead . . . call me names. You know everything about me. I don't need money, 'cause I don't have a family, eh? Well, you don't know anything about me. I'm the one who supports my father. So don't tell me I don't need money. I need it just as much as you. You think I'm crazy, eh? You think it's real funny that I danced at the party like I don't want to dance.

She starts to cry.

What do you want from me . . . anyways? Sure I get nervous. 'Cause . . . I'm . . . the one that Davis wants to get rid of. He can't stand . . . having me around here . . . Every day he's waiting to see me make a mistake. He's looking . . . for an excuse . . . to fire me . . . You'd be nervous, too, if you were in my place. You'd be crazy if you knew how he treated me all these years.

Juanita and Olga both watch her, looking alarmed. Sarah is obviously stunned.

You know what . . . ?

Davis walks into the room. Goldie stops.

DAVIS
Loudly.

Quieten down in here. I could hear you all the way out in the hall.

JUANITA
Hell, this whole place is an accident!

DAVIS
Now, Juanita. Don't get excited.

JUANITA
I ain't excited, man! I ain't excited.

OLGA
Ees very bad fall down, Huguette.

DAVIS
Now if you will just listen to me we can organize ourselves and get back to normal. Look, ladies. An accident like that could happen in any place at any time! It may in fact be very minor.

SARAH
Sure, sure . . . such a minor accident she couldn't move even from her place there on the floor. Oi.

DAVIS
Now, Sarah, please!

JUANITA
Was she talkin' to you out there?

DAVIS
Calm down, Juanita! Let's not make a mountain out of a molehill. As you know, Huguette took a fall. She came running out too quickly and missed her footing. It could happen to anyone. She will be taken to hospital in just a few minutes and she'll be well taken care of.

JUANITA
How bad is she?

DAVIS
What's important is that we must all calm down and carry on with our jobs.
Mimi comes in.

MIMI

Mon dieu, Morton. It's very bad . . . The ambulance men said her leg was broken in a few places . . . that's serious.

DAVIS

Okay, Mimi. We don't need to know all of the clinical details, do we? Just put on your coat fast, and go with her like I told you, and tell them . . .

JUANITA

Wait a minute. Why's Mimi going with her? I mean . . .

DAVIS

Mimi's going because I'm sending her! Believe it or not, I need all my finishers here! Why? Do you want to take an ambulance ride, Juanita?

JUANITA

No . . . I can't stand accidents. But I'm thinking of Huguette. She's hurtin' and I think she might feel better if Sarah goes with her 'cause she knows her best . . .

DAVIS

Well, I say Mimi goes! And I don't want to hear more nonsense about this.

MIMI

Morton . . . Juanita's right, you know. I thought of that too . . . Huguette does not know me very well, ah, and it would be more comfortable for her to go with a friend.

DAVIS

You're my assistant, Mimi, and you're the one who ought to go. Stop paying attention to Juanita.

MIMI

No, no, Morton. It's not that. Me too. I think it's not such a good idea for Huguette. And it makes me

. . . well . . . very uncomfortable too . . . You know, it's strange . . . for me to go.

DAVIS

You just get your coat on now, Mimi, and go out there. Don't talk to me about 'comfortable'. There's one thing you don't understand yet. Your job here is to do what I say! That's all! You don't figure out what's right and wrong . . . You just follow my orders . . . that's all — like everybody else!

MIMI
Stares at him in shock.

I see . . .

DAVIS

Now put your coat on, and get into that ambulance! And tell them exactly what I told you, and . . .

Mimi stares at him for a moment, and then runs out of the room.

Okay. Now can I have your attention here? Goldie, what are you doing?

GOLDIE
At the sink.

I'm taking an aspirin. I have a headache, that's all.

DAVIS

Alright now, ladies. We'll be one worker short this week. I don't know exactly how long Huguette will be away, but she'll probably be away for awhile. I can't train somebody now to do the border stitching in one week. That means we're in even more of a rush this week. And we don't have anymore time to waste. Now take your lunch break, and then back to work. And keep your spirits up. Accidents will happen.

Chuckles.

At least none of you will worry about not having enough work this week. There will be more than enough for all of you. That should keep you happy.
Chuckles again.

JUANITA
Oh hey, that's funny.

DAVIS
What's that, Juanita?

JUANITA
I said that's real funny.

DAVIS
Is something bothering you?

JUANITA
Hell . . . yeah, somethin's botherin' me!

DAVIS
Really?

JUANITA
Yeah, really! This whole scene bothers me! It bothers me that you can make those jokes about us after Huguette's accident! Just 'cause jobs are scarce, you think you can laugh at us like that?

DAVIS
Laugh at you? I'm afraid . . .

JUANITA
Yeah . . . laugh at us. Like 'at least you won't have to worry about coats this week, ladies' . . . like the whole thing was our fault.

DAVIS
Now listen here! I know very well what happened in here. I've seen you people. You don't behave like human beings. I know damned well that you've been picking on Huguette today. And I know damned

well who starts the trouble! It's Goldie! And I'm not going to stand for it much longer.

JUANITA

That ain't what I'm sayin'! Maybe Goldie starts some of the arguing in here, but there's somethin' starting her in the first place. Somethin' always starts all of us off, and that something comes from you, and the way you pay us and the way you treat us.

DAVIS

Now you wait just a minute!

JUANITA

And what bugs me the most is you come out lookin' so bloody white, man — so damned clean. Like you ain't had nothin' to do with this mess at all. Well, you got a lot to do with it, more than I ever seen before.

OLGA

Yah! You make-et trouble for us!

JUANITA

You've been pushin' us around and payin' us a measly damned price for big coats that should pay twice as much. And gettin' us to turn on each other. And . . .

DAVIS

I see . . . Still pecking away at the business of the over-size coats, and I know exactly who put you up to this. Goldie did, and I'm telling you, I am not going to put up with that trouble-maker much longer!

JUANITA

Goldie's got nothin' to do with this one! I'm smart enough to know when I'm getting ripped off! We all are.

OLGA

Yah, yah. Ve not horse, Meester Davis. You make-et us nervous. Ees not goot for us.

DAVIS

I'm not here to talk to you about your nerves! You work out your personal problems at home. When you're in here. You work!

JUANITA

Oh, yeah? Well maybe you're our problem. Maybe it's you who turns us on each other!

OLGA

Yah, ees true!

DAVIS

Wags his finger menacingly at Goldie.

I am warning you, Goldie. I know you're at the bottom of this.

SARAH

Leave Golde alone, Mr. Davis! This didn't come from Golde.

GOLDIE

It's okay, Sarah. Go ahead, Mr. Davis. Try to blame it on me! Why not? I'm the easiest to blame! I stuck here for twenty-one years, so you know you can blame me! 'Goldie starts the trouble!'

DAVIS

You certainly do! You're never satisfied. Ever!

GOLDIE

She stands tall, as though she feels supported by the women. She speaks assertively and clearly, more articulate than ever before.

You want me to smile all the time. Why? Because I started to work here when I was nineteen, and I never once got a raise till the union made you give me a raise?

DAVIS
You got your raise, didn't you?

GOLDIE
You think I should smile 'cause I used to work nights, and you never ever paid me over-time? You think I should pretend I'm happy that when you needed an assistant, you hired somebody else?

JUANITA
Jesus Christ!

GOLDIE
You think I forgot already? You think I don't remember the way you told me not to go to night school 'cause you needed me here to work nights.

DAVIS
Don't you dare blame me for your schooling!

GOLDIE
'What do you need night school for?' you said. 'I need you here, Goldie. You'll work here three nights a week and you'll have a future here.' That's what you said. 'You'll get a promotion, Goldie as soon as the factory gets bigger. Never mind night school. You'll be the first office girl here, Goldie. I promise!'

DAVIS
Enough, Goldie! Nobody's interested!

JUANITA
Hold on, man. We want to hear!

GOLDIE
Shakily continues.
And I listened to you like a fool! I thought you were telling me the truth. A promise is a promise, I thought.

DAVIS
This is ridiculous. I don't need to . . .

GOLDIE
Turns to the women, speaks loudly.
You know how many office girls he hired in here
since I started? Twelve, maybe fifteen. And you
want to know why he didn't give me the job, when
I asked him. 'You didn't go to night school, Goldie,'
he said. 'I need an office girl who went to night
school.'

OLGA
Terrible!

JUANITA
Ain't that a bitch.

DAVIS
You did not have the qualifications.

GOLDIE
No, Goldie's not good enough to be an office girl.
Goldie's just good to sew coats and to scream at.
And now you want to get rid of me, 'cause I'm not
quiet all the time.

DAVIS
I've had it with this talk.

GOLDIE
Explosively.
You know what I gave you? I gave you twenty-one
years of my life!

DAVIS
This is insane!

JUANITA
It don't sound crazy to me.

GOLDIE

And you know what you give me? You laugh at me. Every day, you laugh at me, 'cause you used me good and you know I'm a fool. You know you can start up with me, 'cause I'm here so long, I don't know where to go.

DAVIS

Now, calm down.

GOLDIE

You want me to say I'm satisfied 'cause you lied to me and cheated me. That's what you want. Well I'm not going to smile and say 'thank you'. I know what you promised me, and I know what you did. You can try to blame me, if you want, but you can't. 'Cause I know what you're trying to do now.

DAVIS

That is enough!

JUANITA

She's talkin' the truth.

GOLDIE

Crazy Goldie! I'm not so crazy. I know how you treated me, and now they know too.

In a violent outburst.

And don't think you can scare me anymore with 'I've had it up to here,' 'cause I'm the one who's never been late a day in my life, and never missed a day, and I know my rights. I'm not so stupid. And they all heard me, I have witnesses here! They're on my side. And we all belong to the same union.

The women are stunned, and perfectly silent for a minute.

JUANITA

Damn right.

OLGA

Golda talk goot.

DAVIS

Mimi! . . .Oh, yes, she's at the hospital. Well . . . that was quite a speech. Congratulations! I'm going to have to do something about you first thing in the morning.

JUANITA

I got news for you. We ain't waiting till tomorrow. We're going straight to that union of ours now.

DAVIS

You are going to sit down to work after lunch! I will not allow Goldie to ruin . . .

JUANITA

You can try to put the blame on Goldie, but it won't work, 'cause we are makin' this complaint together, and we won't let you pin nothin' on her. We're goin' to ask for our rights, now, startin' with the price for over-size.

OLGA
Getting ready to go.

Ees not far, union place. Ees one block only! Ve go-et now.

DAVIS

You'll never get away with this! You can't walk out on my time!

JUANITA

This is our lunch break, man! We can do whatever we want with our lunch break!

DAVIS

You'll pay for this!
Davis storms out the door.

OLGA
Scrambling for her boots and coat.
You make-et fast! Golda, put on coat fast.

GOLDIE
Softly.
You told him good, Juanita.

JUANITA
Yeah . . . you did okay yourself, girl.

GOLDIE
I wanted to say that for fifteen years about, but I never had the nerve till today. After you talked, I wasn't scared anymore.

OLGA
Nefer mind now talk-et! Golda! Juanita! Put on coat! Ve go now. Fast!
She sneaks a glance over at Sarah. Sarah is sitting by herself, looking into space as if in a daze.

OLGA
Clearly yearning to reach out to Sarah, nevertheless controls herself and covers up her feelings by busying herself with excessive energy in the task of getting her clothes on, collecting her things and organizing the women, pretending not to be aware of Sarah's presence. She starts putting on her hat, then throws it down again.
Ach! Nefer mind hat! Golda, you take-et purse! Fast!
Finally, Olga calls out to Sarah.
Sarah! Vat you sit now? Ees late! You put on right away coat, yah?
Sarah sits still and looks at her.

SARAH
Dazed.
My . . . coat?

134

OLGA
Speaks very gently.
Sarah . . . Sarooshka, you come-et? Yah?

SARAH
*Looks around very deliberately at the walls of
the garment factory, the racks full of coats — as
though she is analysing the meaning of this
place from a distance now.*
Oi . . . without the people is here nothing with nothing. A few coats, a few hangers, spools of cotton, a
few tables. And from this, people make a whole life.
Forty-years my husband gave . . . Can you imagine?
And me . . .

OLGA
Sarooshka, you come make-et complaint vit us, yah?

SARAH
It's here so quiet all of a sudden . . . no fighting now,
no screaming, no aggravation. It's hard to believe
it's the same place. You see, Olga? Quiet . . . like all
the workers retired already. I don't know myself
what was such an excitement with the factory.

OLGA
Sarooshka, ees late. If not go now to union, ees soon
make-et too late. You come?

SARAH
You think I know? You think I know already what
to do? I know that sometimes a person has to stop.
It comes a time in life when too old is too old. It's
true.

OLGA
Sarooshka, you not old-t! You come better to union
place. Never mind-t old-t!
*Juanita and Golde are moving towards the
door.*

JUANITA

Hey, hurry up, Sarah.

Nervously.

This is for real, girl. C'mon! We can't mess up!

SARAH

Oi, it's true . . . it's important you should go fast. This I know. So . . .

JUANITA

Well, get your coat on, Sarah. We're waitin' for you.

SARAH

Feeling pressured and getting visibly panicky.

Oi, so go already. It's not right you should be late. Noo . . . go already . . .

JUANITA

Well, ain't you comin'? Hell . . . we need you with us. We're gonna look pretty damned stupid . . . just the three of us.

OLGA

Softly and urgently.

You come vit us!

GOLDIE

So are you coming or what, Sarah?

SARAH

Fidgeting with her hands, looking around the room, obviously anxious and unsettled, she gets up slowly and takes her purse in hand. She speaks slowly, softly at first, becoming more and more assertive and certain as she thinks out loud.

What's the right thing to do? I'm not young . . . it's hard already for me . . . Oi, to let you go alone is something funny. A delegation of workers which one worker doesn't come. Tsk! Looks something not right . . . Tsk . . . But after all, if it's time to stop

136

. . . so it's time to stop. But . . . to go home and not say a word—to make like it's not my business altogether? That's . . . uh . . . feh. Not nice! That's for a peasant — not for a worker! Not in a country like this! A long time ago we should have made a complaint! Before Huguette fell! Now . . . it's late . . . But it's better now than not at all, no? No? Sure! Yes! I'm coming! Yes! I have to come! You think I'm going to go home and leave you alone and sit quiet like an old bäbbe which she doesn't have anymore an opinion? Close the door and sit? No! Feh! That's not for me! Plenty time to sit quiet! Plenty time. No! Now it's time to make a complaint the right way, all together, all the workers, like the young immigrant girls from Main Street!

JUANITA
Alright, Sarah! You got it!
    Grabs Goldie, almost pulling her out the door.
Now let's make tracks.

GOLDIE
Shouts.
Ya, hurry up the two of you. We're going out first — so hurry like. Walk fast, eh.
    Juanita and Goldie exit together.

SARAH
Links arms with Olga and starts to follow the other two women, speaking excitedly as she walks.
And if we go on strike, let's say, I'll walk with a little stick too like everybody else. Sure, Olga . . . I'll carry a stick, sure.

OLGA
Holding on to Sarah and picking up speed.
Yah, yah, Sarah.

SARAH

Never mind that Sheila and David will say it's not nice, Olga. What's right is right! And what's right is already nice!

Starts hurrying her pace to keep up with Olga's rhythm of walking.

And if we go on strike, Olga, we'll walk like this — together. We'll hold on one to the other . . . so we won't slip on the ice, God forbid.

Music starts playing the chorus of 'Those Were the Days', as Olga and Sarah walk out of the room together. Lights fade slowly.